Part I

WHY WORKING OUT WORKS

The Fit Factor

How Getting Strong Can Help You Lose Weight

IDG BOOKS WORLDWIDE

AN INTERNATIONAL DATA GROUP COMPANY

Foster City, CA • Chicago, IL • Indianapolis, IN • New York, NY

IDG Books Worldwide
1633 Broadway
New York, NY 10019

A Word About Weight Watchers
Since 1963, Weight Watchers has grown from a handful of people to millions of enrollments annually. Today, Weight Watchers is recognized as the leading name in safe and sensible weight control. Weight Watchers members form a diverse group, from youths to senior citizens, attending meeting virtually around the globe. Weight loss and weight management results vary of individual, but we recommend that you attend Weight Watchers meetings, follow the Weight Watchers food plan and participate in regular physical activity. For the Weight Watchers meeting nearest you, call 1-800-651-6000. Or check out our web site at www.weightwatchers.com.

Weight Watchers Publishing Group
Creative & Editorial Director: Nancy Gagliardi
Senior Editor: Christine Senft, MS
Publishing Assistant: Jenny Laboy-Brace
Editorial Consultant: William D. McArdle, Ph.D.
Text: Daryn Eller, Beryl Meyer
Menu: Jeanne Gedeon, MPH, RD
Illustrations: Michael Gellaty

Library of Congress Cataloging-in-Publication Data

Weight Watchers the fit factor : how getting strong can help you lose weight / Weight Watchers editors
        p.cm.
    Includes index.
    ISBN: 0-02-863704-6
    1. Reducing exercises. 2. Weight loss. 3. Physical fitness for women.
    4. Exercise for women. I. Weight Watchers International.

RA781.6.W45 2000
613.7'045–dc21   00-035088

Manufactured in the United States of America
10 9 8 7 6 5 4 3 2 1

Cover and Book Design by Amy Trombat

Contents

Introduction

ONCE UPON A TIME, WEIGHT WAS CONSIDERED SIMPLY AN ISSUE OF food. But over the last decade, more evidence than ever points to the fact that how much you weigh is closely linked to how much you exercise. Calories count, but so, too, does physical activity.

What's more, exercise can change your life for the better in ways that go beyond your weight. It is the best thing you can do for your overall health and the most effective tool you have against aging. Exercise can make you feel more energetic and less stressed. It can boost your confidence and self-esteem. And, perhaps most importantly, the physical strength you gain through activity can help give you the mental strength needed to take control of your weight and health.

If your commitment to fitness has been spotty, you're not alone. An estimated 60 percent of individuals are sedentary, and the excuses for not exercising are all too familiar—family responsibilities, work pressures, and the general stress of daily life can interfere with even the best of intentions. In addition, some women—particularly those who feel uncoordinated or self-conscious about exercising in front of others—simply find physical activity intimidating.

The good news is that all these excuses are surmountable barriers— but you probably already knew that—so if you're ready to make some serious and long lasting shifts in your exercise routine and lifestyle, nothing can or should stand in your way.

WHY THE PERFECT TIME TO START IS NOW

One of the best things about getting fit is that you can do it at any age. Exercise physiologists around the country have shown, again and again, that even 90-year-olds can benefit from physical activity and, in particular, strength training. As it turns out, it's also true that it doesn't take a Herculean amount of exercise to reap substantial health benefits. One of the most recent studies to drive this encouraging point home was conducted by researchers at Harvard Medical School. Looking at the incidence of heart disease in over 72,000 female nurses 40 to 65 years old, the researchers found that the women who walked briskly for a total of three hours *per week* or exercised vigorously for 90 minutes *per week* had a 30 to 40 percent reduction in risk.

The researchers also determined that even the women who became active later in life had a lower risk of heart disease than women who didn't exercise at all. Consider, too, that late-blooming exercisers also substantially lowered their risk of many other chronic diseases, including diabetes, high blood pressure, osteoporosis, and even some forms of cancer.

There is also another good reason to start exercising now: As you enter your forties and beyond, it becomes increasingly harder to lose weight without exercising. At about 40, the aging process begins in earnest, causing physiological changes that make the body more susceptible to weight gain—so susceptible that if left unchecked, you might gain weight at a rate of ten pounds per decade.

Yet we repeat, the good news is that all these findings are preventable, as long as you take an active role in getting in shape now.

THE FIT FACTOR PLAN

Whether you've been a sporadic exerciser or are someone who is starting from scratch, this book is designed to get you going and guide you toward making exercise a regular habit. We've created an exercise plan that's simple and doable—for a lifetime.

The core of the **Fit Factor Plan** focuses on strength training, an area of fitness that most women neglect. The Plan includes ten simple exercises that, if done properly and regularly, can begin to give you an amazing edge in terms of fitness and weight loss. With this Plan, we're suggesting you start this exercise routine in a slightly different way than you may have in the past. For example, if you've tried walking or joining a gym, only to find yourself a lapsed exerciser within a few months, we suggest you start with strength training. This book clearly explains how embarking on an exercise plan that incorporates weights can have a positive long-term effect on your health as well as your weight loss.

We suggest you focus on the ten strength-training exercises and commit to doing them faithfully. After you've mastered this basic routine, and when you feel you're ready to take on more, we include information on traditional and cutting edge activities that can get you in even better shape. By all means, if you're motivated to try a cardiovascular building routine along with strength training, go right ahead. Even if you've lapsed in the past, be open to exploring a fresh approach to fitness.

Key to your commitment to exercise will be what you learn about how physical activity can make a real difference in your weight, your health, and the way you feel about yourself. And staying committed is essential—not just to losing weight, but to keeping it off since the research shows, again and again, that few people are able to maintain weight loss without exercise.

If you have tried to lose weight before, but without success, put it behind you. You're about to make a positive change that will help you get—and keep—the body you want.

William McArdle, Ph.D.
Professor Emeritus and
Exercise Physiologist
Queens College, New York

one

The Physical Facts

LET'S TALK ABOUT THAT ELUSIVE, maddening topic that probably makes its way into countless conversations you have in a mere week: the condition of your body.

If childhood and the teens are the "wonder" years, the twenties and thirties might best be called the "wonderful" years. These are the decades when your body—no longer developing but not yet in decline—is operating at its peak. It's no accident that most athletes perform their finest feats during their twenties and thirties, or that most women perform theirs—giving birth.

When you are in your twenties and thirties, your bones are dense and strong. You have just the amount of muscle you need to keep your stamina up and your metabolism running at a good rate. Your heart and lungs are working efficiently to send oxygen to your muscles, and your estrogen level is high, insuring that your memory and cognitive skills are in top form. If you exercise during these years, you're probably in even better shape.

Around the time you reach 40, you may begin to notice a few changes in your body, although how quickly and dramatically these changes take place may vary. For instance, consider the woman who goes gray in her thirties and the one who stays gray-free into her sixties. Or the friend who stays thin throughout her life while her best friend puts on several pounds a decade. Or the grandmother who becomes stooped and frail with age and her counterpart who remains strong and vital.

The reasons for these differences can be attributed to two factors: genetics and lifestyle. Scientists know that certain diseases are encoded in a person's individual DNA (your genetic material), but they have also found that other factors that affect your health and well-being are not necessarily written into the script.

Studies, for instance, have found that only 25 to 40 percent of a person's body fat level is attributable to heredity. Research also shows that how you age is only partly due to your parents. In addition, several Swedish studies have looked at differences between both identical and same-sex fraternal twins, only to find that just about 30 percent of physical aging can be attributed to genes. The Swedish studies also show that heredity only accounts for about half of the changes in mental functioning. So, while some things are genetic,

How Healthy Is Your Weight?

It used to be that to figure out if your weight fell into the healthy range, you simply had to check a life insurance table. Now, experts use a measure called the Body Mass Index as a gauge of desirable weight. Your BMI, as it's known, is a single number derived from a formula that assesses weight in relation to height. The higher your BMI, the higher your risk of heart disease, hypertension, diabetes, and many other conditions. Here's how to calculate yours:

1. Multiply weight (in pounds) by 703

2. Multiply height (in inches) by height (in inches)

3. Divide the first number by the second number and round to the nearest whole number to get your BMI.

What your BMI means:

- 18.5 to 24.9—You're in the healthy, normal weight range. As your weight edges up the scale, your risk of disease also increases.

- 25 to 29.9—You're considered overweight and at an increased risk of disease.

- Over 30—You've fallen into the obesity range. This increases your risk of disease the most.

60 to 75 percent of the overall look and health of your body is yours to determine with the right lifestyle choices.

More so than genetics, lifestyle—which includes your levels of activity and stress, as well as what and how much you eat—has a tremendous impact on weight gain and aging. What's more, research shows that the older you get, the *more* lifestyle matters and the *less* genetics does—which means that you can help steer the course your body takes as you grow older. In light of this, consider the following short physiology lesson on the changes that can occur as your body ages.

MUSCLE MATTERS

Muscles are what enable you to scratch an itch and swing a tennis racket. Their condition and size determines how much strength and power you have to engage in these maneuvers. Your muscles take care of so many important functions in your body that it is important to hang on to as much muscle as you possibly can, for as long as you can. Doing so, though, takes a conscious effort because, as you age, muscle (also known as lean body mass) tends to get smaller.

Your muscles are primarily made up of motor units—a combination of muscle fibers, or elongated cells, and the nerves that connect them to your central nervous system. The size of the fibers, which increase with exercise, determines the size of your muscles. The nerves, which communicate with the brain, tell the fibers when to become active, and determine the strength of your muscle's movements.

Although you may start to lose a little muscle in your twenties, real muscle loss generally begins around the time most women turn 40. At that time, individual muscle fibers start to shrink and you may begin to lose whole motor units. (Men, on the other hand, don't begin to substantially lose muscle mass until they're in their fifties and sixties, though researchers are uncertain why there's a gender difference.) One underlying cause of muscle loss may be alterations in the body's hormone levels. Both estrogen and testosterone—the latter a hormone women also produce, though in substantially lower quantities than men—play roles in muscle development. So, as the process slows with age and the body produces less of these hormones with age, it may produce less muscle, too.

Estrogen and Aging

The rise and fall of the hormone estrogen plays a large role in a woman's life, but its effects are especially powerful in her later years.

During menopause (the average age of menopause is 51, give or take a few years), estrogen production declines markedly, speeding up the aging process. Bone loss, for instance, accelerates because estrogen helps facilitate the absorption of dietary calcium and its deposition into bone. Estrogen decline also boosts a woman's risk of heart disease since the hormone helps to inhibit the plaque and cholesterol formations in the arteries which can lead to heart attack.

Another of estrogen's domains is the brain, where it promotes the growth of brain cells and helps foster the transmission of neurons. With less estrogen in circulation, memory and information processing are affected; some research now suggests that there may even be a link between estrogen and the development of Alzheimer's disease.

Some evidence also suggests that estrogen plays a role in age-related weight gain, although scientists aren't really sure why. Nonetheless, a study conducted at the Massachusetts Institute of Technology, which looked at the effect of menopause on both obese and nonobese women, had some edifying results. As many as 64 percent of the nonobese women included in the study gained an average of 15 to 20 pounds after menopause. Ninety-six percent of those who were obese also gained, weighing in with an average of 21 to 23 extra pounds. Research also indicates that women not only gain weight during menopause, but that they begin to gain more in their abdominal area.

Estrogen plays such a large role in health and well-being that many women are turning to hormone replacement therapy (HRT) as they reach the menopausal years. If you are near or approaching menopause you should have your doctor speak to you about your health factors and possible options.

Some of this deterioration of muscle—called sarcopenia—is natural. Yet for most women, the primary cause of muscle loss is inactivity. Research shows that if you don't use muscle, you lose it. Consider, for example, that in a Baylor College of Medicine study which looked at the effect of bed rest on men, researchers found that the men lost between 8.5 and 4.6 pounds of lean body mass—mostly in their lower body—during 17 weeks of limited mobility. The study makes a sobering point of just how easy it is for muscles to deteriorate.

How easy is easy? Consider this: Since 1958, researchers have been contributing to the ongoing Baltimore Longitudinal Study on Aging, a project devoted to observing many aspects of aging in over 2,000 people. According to the study's data, the average woman will lose 20 to 25 percent of her muscle mass from her forties until her eighties—that translates to about $1/3$ of a pound of muscle a year. During early menopause, a woman might even lose more muscle; the research suggests as much as a pound a year.

Over the years, as muscle mass declines, so does strength and power. On average, an inactive woman may see a 12 percent decline in her upper-body strength and a 14 percent decline in her lower-body strength per decade. Interestingly, as you age you lose more strength in your legs than you lose in your torso, while men surrender strength symmetrically. Ultimately, though, both men and women who do nothing to stop muscle loss appear to suffer the same fate: They end up about half as strong at age 80 as they were when they were 40.

BONES OF CONTENTION

Long after your body stops growing, your bones continue to be in flux. Most people continue to add bone mass up until their twenties, reaching peak bone mass—that point at which the bones are their strongest—in their thirties. But even when your bones are at their most dense, they're far from static. Rather, bones continually break themselves down, then build themselves back up again, a cyclical process known as remodeling.

Your bones are composed of a combination of the protein collagen and several minerals including calcium, phosphate, and, in smaller amounts, sodium, magnesium, and potassium. Remodeling occurs when blood levels of calcium drop and the body "borrows" calcium from the bones to aid in, among other things, regulating heart rate and muscle contractions. When calcium becomes available again, the bones reabsorb the mineral, insuring that bones stay solid and healthy.

As long as you're getting adequate calcium in your diet and using your muscles and bones, this process works pretty efficiently. If your calcium intake is frequently low, or you live a sedentary life, your body will keep making withdrawals from your bones, but the bones won't be able to rebuild themselves. Eventually, they'll weaken and become fragile.

Even if your calcium intake is beyond reproach, however, you're likely to experience some bone loss with age. Around the age of 35, the mineral content of a woman's bones begins to decrease by about one percent a year. Then, because estrogen plays a role in aiding calcium absorption, a menopausal dip in the hormone causes the rate of bone loss to accelerate to two to three percent per year during the five to ten years after menopause. Some women—those genetically predisposed to osteoporosis—stand to lose much more. (Men can also get osteoporosis, but there's a dramatic gender difference: About 80 percent of the people who have the disease are women.)

How much bone you lose over the years also has to do with your lifestyle and activity level. Smokers tend to lose more bone because smoking causes the body to excrete (rather than use) calcium. Heavy drinkers are also at a higher risk because they often don't get enough calcium or vitamin D, which helps the body absorb calcium.

Sedentary types, however, lose bone for an entirely different reason. Exercise creates what's known as mechanical stress on the bones. When the muscles tug on them at an intensity that's greater than, say, reaching for the remote control or walking into the kitchen, the bones respond by building themselves up to handle the stress—physiologists refer to this as the overload principle. When there's little or no stress on the bones, they easily breakdown. Bone loss, in fact, is one of the risks astronauts face because of their marked decrease of activity combined with the weightlessness (lack of gravity) that generally reduces the stress on their muscles in space.

A SHIFT IN BODY SHAPE

If you're like most woman, you're probably pear-shaped; that is, your body tends to store fat in your hips and thighs. Men, on the other hand, are more likely to store fat in the abdominal region, making

Three Dos and Don'ts of Healthy Bones

❋ **Do eat calcium rich foods.** Low-fat dairy products are obvious choices, but also consider vegetables such as figs, broccoli, turnip and mustard greens, watercress, and bok choy (although spinach and Swiss chard are high in calcium they aren't well absorbed by the body).

❋ **Don't engage in very low-calorie diets.** A diet comprised of less than 800 calories a day leads to muscle and bone loss. In fact, when you lose weight by diet alone (that is, without adding any exercise into the equation), as much as 25 to 30 percent of your loss may be in the form of lean body mass (which includes both muscle and bone). The result is both unhealthy (you can set yourself up for osteoporosis) and self-defeating (when you lose muscle you burn fewer calories at rest, making it hard to drop weight).

❋ **Do choose calcium-fortified foods.** Consider orange juice (which, ounce for ounce, has the same amount of calcium as milk), some ready-to-eat cereals, and low-fat frozen desserts (check that the label claims to provide at least 25 percent of the Daily Value for calcium—and watch your portions).

them look more like apples. But around the time of menopause, many women who have always been pears start to store fat around their middles and, as with most physical changes women begin to experience around midlife, the behind-the-scenes culprit is estrogen.

As estrogen production begins to drop off, it changes the activity of an enzyme in fat tissue called lipoprotein lipase (LPL). One of LPL's jobs is to usher fat into the cells where it's stored and, during middle age, it begins directing fat to the body's middle. So even if you were always a pear, you may begin to take on a more apple shape.

To give you an idea of how much belly fat women are capable of gaining in their later years, consider a study conducted at the University of Alabama. Using an imaging tool that allowed them to view a cross section of the abdomen, researchers found those women ages 20 to 40 had an average of 55 square centimeters of abdominal fat. Women ages 55 to 80 had twice that—an average of 110 square

Assessing Your Risk

Although BMI (Body Mass Index—to calculate yours, see box on page 4) is considered a good indicator of risk, be aware that it doesn't tell the whole story. Location of body fat can make a difference in your risk. Measure the circumference of your waist just above the navel: A circumference of 30 inches or more doubles your risk of heart disease; a waist measurement of 38 inches triples it.

For another, more precise, way to calculate your waist-hip ratio, consider the following calculation:

1. Measure your waist with a tape measure: (a)

2. Measure the fullest part of your hips/buttocks: (b)

3. Divide (a) by (b) which equals (c), your waist-hip ratio.

For a woman, a number greater than 0.8 indicates a higher than average risk. For men, that number is 0.95. If your number indicates risk, speak with your physician.

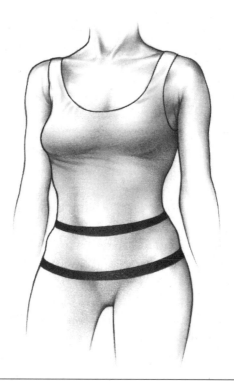

centimeters of fat stored in the belly. Without any intervention from hormone replacement therapy (HRT), diet, or exercise, some women may end up with double the amount of abdominal fat as they move into their later years.

CARDIOVASCULAR CONCERNS

As you read this, your lungs, heart, and blood vessels (the latter two are known as your cardiovascular system) are engaged in the fairly simple process of feeding your body with oxygen. When you breathe in, tiny capillaries take the oxygen from your lungs and transfer it into your bloodstream. Your heart then pumps the oxygenated blood through your blood vessels to your muscles and other tissues that need it for energy. When you exert yourself, your body will speed up the process in order to accelerate the transfer of oxygen from your lungs to your working muscles (that's why you breathe harder and your heart beats faster when you, say, walk at a brisk pace or pump the pedals on a bike).

Just *how* hard you breathe and how fast your heart beats when you work to accomplish those feats is a sign of your aerobic capacity, or the ability of your body to distribute and use oxygen within a given time. Aerobic capacity is sometimes called cardiovascular fitness and, in the parlance of exercise physiologists, maximum oxygen consumption or VO_2max (the volume of oxygen consumed per minute). If you have good aerobic capacity, you will barely feel your heart pound when you walk or bike; if you have poor aerobic capacity, you will feel overtaxed and out of breath with just moderate exercise.

Men have a greater aerobic capacity than women do because they naturally possess less body fat, which does not contribute to oxygen consumption in exercise, but both sexes suffer a decline in their oxygen-processing function with age. This fact is especially true if you're not moving much: Between the ages of 25 to 30, sedentary people generally experience a 9 to 15 percent decrease in aerobic capacity per decade.

Since genetics plays a role in determining aerobic capacity, some people end up with less heart and lung power than others. But even with heredity on your side, if you're inactive, your aerobic capacity may diminish due to a natural slowdown in your heart's capacity to pump blood. Muscle loss just exacerbates the problem. Since muscle tissue depends on oxygen for energy, the less muscle you have, the less demand there will be on your cardiovascular system. This point is important because the only way you can increase your aerobic capacity is to make demands on your cardiovascular system. If you're sedentary, it's already under-worked; losing muscle will just make it worse because that decreases your ability to exercise.

THE FLEXIBILITY FACTOR

Are you flexible if you can touch your toes? Well, yes and no. Some people are flexible all over, while others are more flexible in some areas of the body than they are in others. Flexibility refers to the ability of the muscles and connective tissue to "give" combined with the joints' ability to allow for a good range of motion. In the case of touching your toes, your flexibility would depend on whether your hamstrings and the muscles in your lower back are elastic enough to allow you to stretch your upper body toward the floor. Even if you can touch your toes, it doesn't mean your arms will be limber enough to allow you to reach up and grab something off a high shelf.

Whatever your degree of flexibility is now, you stand to lose some of it as you grow older. Flexibility hasn't been studied extensively, but researchers believe that it decreases with age because, as you get older, your body tissues lose fluid, which makes them less supple and resilient. Other changes also take place in the connective tissue—including tendons, which attach muscle to bone, and ligaments, which adjoin bone to bone. They become tauter, restricting muscle movement and altering the bones' alignment so the joints' range of motion becomes limited.

It's difficult to gauge just how much flexibility you surrender with age, but if you've ever seen an elderly person walking stiffly—or even felt stiffness and inhibited in movement yourself—you have some idea of how great the loss can be.

THINKING DIFFERENT?

Who hasn't been able to remember the name of a favorite actor or a frequently-dialed phone number? Just about everyone, even people in their twenties, has memory lapses, and these frustrating moments tend to increase with age. Simultaneously, the speed at which you process information generally ebbs as does reaction time, such as the time it takes to do something like step on the brakes.

A person starts experiencing a decline in some mental abilities at about age 50. While experts still are not quite sure why this happens, it most likely has to do with a natural loss of brain cells and lowered production of the hormones that affect neurological connections. Although inactivity has never been implicated in memory loss or lowered cognitive functioning, the good news is there is a connection between exercise and increased mental agility.

two

Weighty Matters

A FEW YEARS AGO, scientists at the National Center for Health Statistics (NCHS) published a report illustrating what happens to many Americans as they age. According to the NCHS's third National Health and Nutrition Examination Survey (NHANESIII), conducted from 1988 to 1994, the average person gains close to ten pounds of unwanted fat a decade. At that rate, a woman who starts out at 130 pounds when she's 20, will wind up weighing as much as 160 by the time she's 50.

Yet the total weight picture is not as bleak as the numbers would suggest. For instance, you have to consider how genetics fit into the health picture. Thanks to the recent work of obesity researchers, we know that genetics do indeed play a role in body weight. However, researchers have also found that there are *many* factors that contribute to weight gain; heredity is only one piece of the puzzle.

The fact remains that no one is destined to gain weight continually as she or he grows older. Many Americans *do* put on pounds as they age, but you can take preventive measures to make sure that doesn't happen to you. In fact, if you exercise and watch what you eat in earnest, it's possible not only to slim down now—no matter what your age—but to also *stay* slim later in life.

OF FAT GENES AND THIN ONES

Fatness and thinness run in families. For instance, children who have one or more obese parents have double the risk of becoming obese themselves. Genetics also determines the shape of a person's body. It is no accident that some family members' bodies look like carbon copies of one another.

Clearly, there also is a genetic component in your propensity to lose and gain weight. One way that researchers have shown this to be true is by looking at what happens when identical twins change their overall calorie balance. When the twins increased their calorie-burning through exercise, both lost approximately the same amount of body fat. Likewise, when they increased their calorie intake by eating more, they each gained in equal measure. Correspondingly, a study conducted at Laval University in Quebec found some people had stored up to 200 calories per day more than others on the same diet and exercise plan. It's no wonder, then, that there are women who can eat uninhibitedly without repercussion, while others must reign in their appetites if they hope to stay slim.

What accounts for these differences? Not just one gene, it seems, but several. Some thinner people, for instance, inherit genes that make them fidgeters and fidgeting, benign as these small movements appear, can actually burn off as much as 800 calories a day.

Genes also play a role in determining a person's appetite. One gene in particular, the obesity gene—or Ob-gene—indirectly affects hunger by controlling the fat cells' production of a hormone called leptin. Leptin's job is to inform the brain that the fat cells are adequately supplied so that it can regulate the appetite and metabolism—the rate at which you burn calories—accordingly. When the fat cells become "full," they release leptin into the bloodstream. The hormone is then transported to the hypothalamus—the brain's appetite and metabolism control center—where, through interaction with brain chemicals, it dampens hunger and keeps the metabolism moving at a steady clip.

Unfortunately, this elegant metabolic- and appetite-regulating process doesn't work efficiently for everybody. For some people, their Ob-gene hampers their fat cells' production of leptin. Others have a predisposition that reduces the brain chemical's sensitivity to leptin. In either case, the brain doesn't get the message that the body has enough fat stored away to prevent hunger. Thus, it keeps the appetite up and the metabolism down.

Scientists have also isolated another gene that affects a person's weight. Called Uncoupling Protein-2 (UCP2) and produced in every tissue of the body, this gene causes a rise in metabolism. Researchers speculate that those people who seem to eat endlessly and never gain an ounce may have a high level of UCP2 activity going on in their bodies.

There is a racial component that may also be playing a role in your size. African-American women have a higher rate of obesity than Caucasian women, a fact which has long been blamed on cultural differences in eating and exercise habits. However, recent research indicates that there may be inherited physiological characteristics that account for the discrepancy. In 1997, a University of Pennsylvania Medical School study found that obese African-American women burned nearly 100 calories fewer per day while at rest than obese Caucasian women. A later study by the same researchers found that African-American women also suffer a greater drop in metabolism than Caucasian women after weight loss, an outcome which may make it even more difficult for African-American women to keep lost pounds from creeping back.

Although genetics seem to be at work here as well, the effect of heredity on body weight must be kept in perspective. Only about 25 to 40 percent of factors affecting obesity are attributable to heredity. There are still many components of body weight that are well within your control.

IS THERE A NATURAL "SET POINT"?

If you've ever tried to lose weight before, you might be able to identify with this scenario: You go on a diet and see fairly quick results. The first 10 or 15 pounds come off pretty easily, but then you begin to plateau. Your weight loss slows to a crawl—or even comes to a complete halt. Before you know it, you've gained back every pound that you'd lost, almost to the ounce.

Some scientists have a name for the mechanism behind this phenomenon: the set point. The set point theory suggests that most individuals have a predetermined weight at which your body feels most comfortable and to which it will stubbornly cling. Lose

Profile in Fitness

NAME: JUDY B.

OCCUPATION: COMPUTER PROGRAMMER

HOME STATE: NEW YORK

AGE: 44 YEARS OLD

BEFORE WEIGHT: 276 LBS

AFTER WEIGHT: 153 LBS

HEIGHT: 5'6"

HOW SHE STAYS STRONG AND FIT:

WALKING, 4 TIMES PER WEEK

SWIMMING, EVERY WEEKEND, 2 HOURS PER DAY

❁

"If you put your mind to something, hold onto your inner strength and just stay focused, you can accomplish anything."

As an adult, my weight has spiraled and yo-yoed time and again. Over the past 20 years, I've probably lost—and regained—a total of 100 pounds. When I was very heavy, I swam a lot—four hours a weekend year-round. It gave me a feeling of weightlessness and freedom that I didn't experience anywhere else.

Losing weight on Weight Watchers has enabled me to enjoy walking again. It was very difficult to move around when I was heavy. I first started walking in increments—about a half-mile to a mile. Then I added some walking to my commute to work, getting off public transportation a block or two before my office. Gradually, I increased the frequency and length—walking four times a day, including my entire lunch hour.

I joined the New York Roadrunners Club and started going to their activities, which average about ten miles per recreational event. Instead of running, though, I walk. I've injured my ankles numerous times—I have metal screws in one of them after I tore the ligaments—so I often use a cane for support.

Last November, I walked the New York City Marathon—a total of 26 miles—in nine and a half hours. At first, I didn't think I had the guts to *do it. The last three and a half hours, I was in pain every step of the way. But I just kept thinking, "This is what I've done so far; this is what I still need to do." All I knew was that I was going to walk away with the medal given to every marathoner who crosses the finish line. And I did— one of the last of the ambulatory participants to do so. Stepping over that line, I was totally exhilarated and felt empowered, like I could do anything.*

What I've learned—and have been able to model for my children— is that if you put your mind to something, hold on to your inner strength and don't worry about anything—just stay focused—you can accomplish anything.

weight—or gain it—and your body will do all it can to get back to its original condition.

The set point, experts contend, is a holdover from more primitive times; a survival mechanism designed to help you conserve your fat stores when food is scarce. Of course, food isn't scarce in most parts of the world now, but the body can't distinguish between a drought and a diet: Any time you restrict calories and subsequently shed pounds, your brain compares your body's actual weight to its preferred weight, then tries to close the gap.

How, exactly, the body does this is not quite clear. Researchers suspect that one way your body compensates is by increasing your appetite. As you lose weight and your fat cells shrink in size, they release less leptin, the hormone that puts a damper on hunger. This process makes it even more difficult to stay on a reduced-calorie regimen—and may be the reason so many people trying to lose weight eventually quit.

Another way bodies may fight back when confronted with weight loss is by increasing the level of the fat-storing enzyme lipoprotein lipase. Because lipoprotein lipase is produced in the fat cells, a fatter person will produce more of the enzyme and, consequently, store more fat. Unfortunately, this can make shedding pounds an even bigger struggle for those who need to lose weight the most.

What may compound the problem, some researchers suspect, is the fact that weight loss also causes the body—again, in an attempt to conserve fat—to slow down its metabolism. And the slowdown can be substantial enough to grind weight loss to a halt—or even cause a dieter to gain back some of what was already lost.

In a 1995 study, researchers at Rockefeller University in New York City looked at the effects of weight changes on the metabolisms of 23 normal-weight individuals. The people who lost 10 percent of their body weight on an 800-calorie-a-day diet also decreased their metabolisms by 10 percent. Notably, the researchers also looked at what happened when the subjects gained 10 percent *more* body weight. They, too, experienced a shift in metabolism—only their calorie-burning rates *increased* by 10 percent.

Not all experts agree that the Rockefeller study's results are conclusive, however. They argue that, while the metabolic rate may slow

Is it a No-No to Yo-Yo?

Even if, in the past, you have yo-yoed—repeatedly lost and gained weight—don't worry. Evidence now suggests that yo-yoing doesn't create as much damage as once thought.

Originally, experts theorized that going on and off diets would slow the body's metabolism, create a greater preference for fatty foods, cause greater weight gain in the abdominal area, and make it progressively more difficult to lose weight the next time around. After further study, that theory has essentially been deemed obsolete. Yo-yo dieting, the latest thinking has it, has no long-term physiological effects.

This isn't to say that losing and regaining weight can't take an emotional toll on your psyche. It can be dispiriting and make it harder to get motivated to try again; that's why the best strategy is to find an eating and exercise regime you can live with, then adhere to it. Still, it's heartening to know that, even if you've yo-yoed in the past, there's no physiological reason you can't lose weight now. If you truly feel you're ready to lose weight, don't let past experiences stand in your way or be an excuse for why you shouldn't lose weight now.

after calories are reduced, it will rise back up to a normal pace. In recent years, in fact, a small but growing group of researchers are beginning to question if the set point theory really exists. Thus, they're not certain if metabolism is as big a culprit in determining set point as has been previously thought, so it is something to consider, though it may not hold as much weight as previously thought.

On the bright side, you're not condemned to live with the set point nature gave you. Evidence suggests that careful eating and regular exercise can lower your set point. In chapter 4, we'll discuss how.

THE MUSCLE-METABOLISM CONNECTION

One of the great myths about the human body is that muscle turns to fat if you don't exercise. The truth is, muscle cells can't be converted to fat cells or vice versa. But there is a connection between muscle and body fat. When you lose muscle, it doesn't turn to fat, but it does make you more likely to *gain* fat. In fact, some experts attribute much of the ten-pound-a-decade weight gain experienced by sedentary Americans to muscle loss.

Here's how it works: Fat tissue doesn't do much, but muscle tissue does. Muscles are continually active, and to keep them fueled, you must burn calories constantly—even while you're at rest. This physiological fact keeps your metabolism in high gear, and the more muscle you have, the more calories it will ensure that you burn.

Consider what happens when you begin to lose muscle: Over time, your resting energy needs will diminish, but you're not likely to be aware of it. Like many people, you'll probably go on eating as you always have, only to end up taking in more calories than you're able to burn. Faced with excess energy from food, your body will store it as fat. It's not your muscles that have turned to fat, but by shrinking, they've caused you to pack more of it away in your existing fat cells.

The metabolic decline that comes from muscle loss occurs gradually. On average, a sedentary person's metabolism decreases at a rate of 2 to 3 percent per decade starting at the age of 20, which translates into about 100 fewer calories per day with each passing decade. It may not seem like much now—what's an ounce of cheese or a slice and a

Metabolic Musings

To make sure your metabolism stays revved and your hunger kept in check, you must eat regular, sensible meals and be sure to eat at least as many calories as your body burns at rest. Meal skipping is a surefire way to wreak havoc on your metabolism, so if you know you may be in a situation where getting a meal may be an issue, plan ahead. You can easily remedy the problem by getting in the habit of always carrying a piece or two of fruit (like apples, pears, or bananas) in your bag. If you find you are skipping breakfast or lunch, try preparing a few bagels with spreadable fruit in the evenings. Keep them wrapped tightly and in your refrigerator so they are waiting to be snatched up in your frantic morning rush. A made-the-night-before lean turkey sandwich also helps offset skipping lunch or dinner. If you tend to eat on the go frequently, individually packaged items, like cereal, pretzels, low-fat cheese wedges, and low-fat crackers always should be at the ready, too.

half of bread less per day?—but those 100 calories add up: A woman who was able to maintain her weight at 2,000 calories a day when she was 20, will only be able to eat 1,600 calories a day when she's 60.

Yet that may only be true for people who don't exercise. Studies show that people who engage in regular strength training and aerobic exercise are able to resist the slowdown in resting metabolism that usually comes with aging. That is, by maintaining muscle through strength-training and burning extra calories through aerobic exercise, it's possible to prevent weight gain as you grow older.

WHY YOU NEED TO BREAK THE CYCLE OF INACTIVITY

You know that losing strength, cardiovascular fitness, bone density, and flexibility over the years will adversely affect your health. Less obvious is the fact that losing fitness will also affect your weight by reducing your stamina. Without the stamina you need to do the day-to-day tasks that burn calories, you're likely to put on pounds.

Even if you don't engage in a regular exercise routine, you probably engage in many physical activities during your day. Whether it's walking up stairs or gardening, it's still activity. But the less fit you are, the more uncomfortable these tasks will feel. So you may find yourself driving instead of walking, or leaving the gardening to your spouse or the gardener. In the end, you'll not only decrease your daily energy expenditure, you'll lose even more fitness. Inactivity breeds more inactivity, creating a vicious cycle.

In addition to loss of strength, declining aerobic capacity can also make you more inclined to stay on the couch. When you must huff and puff to get oxygen to your working muscles, just crossing the street can seem a workout in itself. The same holds true when you lose flexibility; you may find simple tasks like bending down to lift something off the floor can leave you feeling stiff and uncomfortable.

Flexibility makes moving through your daily routine easier—and a whole lot safer. Some evidence also suggests that poor flexibility can make you more susceptible to injury, particularly in areas of the body like the Achilles tendon (located just above the heel) and the hamstrings (the muscles in the back of the thighs). Say, for example, that you slip on a rug, then extend your leg to catch yourself before you fall. If your leg muscles aren't elastic enough to meet the demand, those muscles may strain, or even tear.

Strong bones are as important as flexibility. Severe bone loss leading to osteoporosis makes a woman susceptible to fractures—and it's not just the elderly who are at risk. By age 60, the bones of some women become brittle enough to break easily. Needless to say, a fracture can sideline you from activity, exacerbating the weakness of your bones, and possibly lead to weight gain.

Again, exercise offers a solution. By becoming fit, you can even help reverse the cycle, and you'll have the energy and confidence to take on even more physical challenges.

EXTRA POUNDS AND YOUR PERIOD

If you're like many women, you probably experience some weight gain at certain times during your menstrual cycle. Thankfully, however, these extra pounds are usually temporary. If you feel bloated right before and during you're period it's because hormonal fluctuations cause the

Prepping for PMS

Researchers have made inroads in terms of pinpointing and quelling premenstrual syndrome (PMS). In order to assess whether or not you truly have PMS, you must keep a log, noting the who, what, when, and where of any significant physical shifts in your body or mood swings (for greater accuracy, keep the diary for two consecutive months). If you feel the hormones may be playing a role in your life, consider the following:

- Drink water, which can help reduce any bloating by helping flush the excess sodium from your body.

- Lower your caffeine, sugar, and alcohol intakes.

- Eat smaller meals throughout your day to curb increased hunger.

- Be physically active—exercise can help reduce stress and stabilize hormones.

kidneys to retain salt and water. In fact, you may put on anywhere from one to six pounds of water weight, but it will eventually dissipate.

Less likely to dissipate are the additional calories many women eat when they're at the premenstrual stage of their cycles. But research shows that the body compensates for the extra calories by boosting its metabolism. In a recent study conducted at Pennsylvania State University, investigators had 20 women ages 20 to 34 eat all their meals and snacks for three days in a lab during the beginning and the end of two consecutive menstrual cycles. As expected, the women did increase their food intake in the premenstrual phase, but it turned out that they also burned more calories. In the end, they did not put on any extra pounds. (Notably, the researchers also looked at the women's taste preferences and they showed no greater interest than usual in chocolate or other sweets.)

Another topic the Penn State researchers investigated was whether contraceptives make a difference in a woman's weight. Many people believe that contraceptive hormones increase the appetite and slow the metabolism, causing weight gain. But when the same women repeated the earlier protocol—this time after being injected with a contraceptive called Depo-Provera—they showed no change in hunger, the rate at which they burned calories, or in their body weight. Depo-Provera, the researchers concluded, doesn't cause weight gain. Other studies have also shown that oral contraceptives do not cause weight gain either.

three

Exercising Off Weight

MANAGING YOUR WEIGHT THROUGHOUT YOUR LIFE can be enough of a challenge without having to worry about the effects of aging and risk of disease. Take solace, though, in the fact that you don't need a different strategy to address each of these issues. If you work out regularly and eat a nutritious, moderate diet, you can check off a laundry list of health rewards for your efforts.

Consider, for instance, that as you strengthen your muscles, you'll also be strengthening your bones and boosting your metabolic rate. As you condition your heart and lungs, you will improve your body composition, your mood, and even your memory.

What's more, you also will drop pounds. Researchers have found that physical activity changes the interior architecture of the body, making it easier to lose weight and keep it off. Although it was once believed that only aerobic exercise (the kind that gets your heart rate up for a minimum of 20 to 30 minutes) did the trick, the latest developments in exercise science suggest that strength training also can make a notable contribution to the cause.

Even if your primary reason for exercising is to shed pounds, you'll be glad to know that you're also getting some substantial health perks in the process. Physical activity, experts now say with certainty, is part of the cure for just about everything that ails Americans; it's even prescribed for maladies such as heart disease and backaches that were once thought best remedied by bed rest.

Although Americans are not known for having the leanest diet in the world, experts contend inactivity is still the primary cause of America's weight problem. Consider the evidence that if you exercise, you'll probably have a leaner body: Studies show that people who weigh in with the least amount of extra pounds and most favorable distribution of body fat have higher levels of physical activity than their overweight peers. They also show that exercisers have the most success at losing weight and, perhaps even more importantly, at keeping it off. What's more, active people don't gain as much weight with age as their sedentary peers.

While watching what you eat also plays an important role in weight loss, it helps you slim down in just one way: by reducing your calorie intake. But the manner in which exercise works is more complex; it helps you shed pounds (and maintain weight loss) in several ways. Here are five of them.

1. **Tipping the energy balance.** The mechanics of weight loss are simple: If you expend more calories than you consume, your body will dip into its fat stores for fuel and you will shed pounds. While this is a relatively simple process, it does take a fairly substantial gap between energy in and energy out (for example, you need to burn 3,500 additional calories) before you can shed one pound.

   The truth is, unless you just have a few pounds to lose, it's difficult to lose weight just by exercising. But when it's used as an adjunct to healthful eating, physical activity can contribute greatly to helping you achieve a calorie deficit. For instance, by taking a brisk hour-long walk, the average 150-pound woman burns about 366 calories. Multiply that by six and you've burned close to an extra 2,200 calories per week. What's more, some people experience what's called the "after-burn" effect of exercise: a small jump in their metabolic rate that lasts several hours following 45 minutes or more of aerobic exercise.

   Becoming a regular exerciser can also help you change your mind-set about physical activity. As you build stamina, you may be more likely to add little bouts of exercise to your day by, say, climbing stairs instead of taking elevators,

Won't Exercise Make Me Hungrier?

You work out on the treadmill for a half-hour, then head for a restaurant to have dinner. Famished, you dive into the bread basket and order three courses. What's going on?

Well, one thing is certain: It *wasn't* the exercise that made you hungry.

Scientific evidence looking at physical activity's effect on appetite indicates that most people don't end up eating more calories when they exercise. Some research even suggests that overweight people actually experience a decrease in appetite post-workout.

Yet, there are some food-related pitfalls of exercise. If every time you complete a good workout you feel you should reward yourself with a piece of cake, you're not going to lose weight. Likewise, if you overestimate how much energy you expend during a workout and end up eating more than you've burned, you may even put on pounds. The bottom line: Listen to your body. If it's not telling you it's hungry, don't feed it.

pacing while you talk on the phone, or getting off the bus a few stops early. All this extra calorie-burning will add up, helping you to increase your calorie deficit even more.

2. **Building calorie-hungry muscle.** Another way you can burn more calories is to strength train. Although you only burn a nominal amount of calories while engaged in lifting weights, regular strength training will increase your muscle mass and, in turn, will increase your metabolism (oftentimes substantially). A study conducted by researchers at the Jean Mayer USDA Human Nutrition Research Center on Aging at Tufts University, found that women who lifted weights increased their calorie-burning level by an average of 300 calories a day.

There's no age limit to increasing your muscle mass either. Older people can make as significant a gain in lean body tissue as people who are half their age. If you're at an age where you've already lost muscle, this means you can restore some of what you've forfeited—and stop any further degeneration.

Living (But Not Looking) Large

Many women fear that by building muscle, they will also be building bulk. The truth is, for a woman to transform herself into the Incredible Hulk takes an intense regimen of heavy weight lifting and special diet. Moderate weight-training programs (like the one in this book) don't build bulk—but they do build strength, and firm and tone muscles.

By increasing your strength, you will find it much easier to accomplish other physical activities. In 1994, Tufts University researchers found that previously sedentary women who strength trained two days a week for a year began living 27 percent more active lives. Strength training will not only help you burn more calories by raising your metabolism, it will give you the energy you need to engage in other forms of fitness, too.

Another reason why you would want to include strength training: When you cut back on too many calories and you don't exercise, you lose not just fat, but muscle and bone. The loss of muscle decreases your metabolism and makes it harder to shed pounds; the loss of bone can set you up for osteoporosis. If you exercise, you'll preserve both muscle and bone (and cause more of your weight to be fat loss); keep all your calorie-hungry, lean body mass intact; and decrease your risk of ending up with brittle bones.

3. **Increasing fat burning.** When you engage in aerobic exercise, your body has a choice of energy stores to choose from: your muscle tissue, which banks digested carbohydrates in the form of glycogen; and your fat cells, which warehouse fat. Ultimately, the body draws on both glycogen and fat for energy. But as you become fitter, the balance tips towards fat because the body becomes better at mobilizing the fat in and out of its fat depots. At the same time, the muscles get better at converting the fat into usable energy.

4. **Making dieting and weight maintenance easier.** If you were to rely on cutting calories alone, you'd have to reduce your intake by 3,500 calories a week just to lose one pound. Add exercise to the equation, though, and you don't have to cut back as rigidly to get the same results. Say, for instance, that you trim 200 calories from your diet each day, walk three days a week for an hour (about 366 calories burned per session) and take an aerobics class two other days (burning about 420 calories per session). In total, this regimen adds up to a weekly calorie decrease of approximately 1,938. Throw in the metabolism-boosting effect of strength training and you achieve a net calorie deficit of over 4,000 calories, or slightly more than a pound, per week.

Just as combining diet and exercise may be the best way to lose weight, a growing body of evidence suggests that it's also the best way to keep it off. One of the most recent research projects to shed light on preventing weight regain is the National Weight Control Registry, a study of nearly 2,000 people (80 percent of them women), ages 34 to 55, who've been able to maintain weight loss long-term. The participants had several strategies for keeping the pounds off, but one of the secrets to their success was staying physically active.

Putting the Spot-Reducing Myth to Rest

Will doing a thousand abdominal crunches whittle away your middle? Will leg lifts melt fat off your thighs? Unfortunately, no. Although exercises aimed at specific body parts help tone and strengthen the muscles in that area, they won't necessarily reduce more fat from those parts. Aerobic exercise will help you achieve a calorie deficit, causing your body to dip into its fat reserves. Although you can't direct from where the fat is drawn, it will generally come from the areas with the greatest deposits. On the bright side, overall weight loss can help reduce problem areas, and a fitter stronger body can give you a great sense of confidence in your physique.

5. **Helping prevent weight-loss plateaus.** When the body is deprived of incoming calories, it defends itself by lowering its metabolism, which can make weight loss slow to a crawl. But regular exercise seems to out-maneuver the body's self-defense mechanism by helping to keep the metabolism operating at a normal level. In a University of California, Davis, study, for instance, five people were fed a 500-calorie diet for four weeks, causing their metabolic rates to drop 87 percent the first two weeks. However, when they began exercising during the second two weeks, their metabolic rates reversed themselves, returning to their pre-dieting levels. (Although experts are not quite sure what causes this reversal of fortune, some believe it may have to do with changes in hormonal levels that occur with exercise.)

As you build muscle, they will burn more calories, which will counter the metabolic slowdown that comes from dieting. Some researchers suspect that exercise resets the body's "set point" (preferred weight) as well. This isn't to say that working out can change a person who has an innately curvaceous figure into someone with an angular physique, but it may allow you to get past a weight to which your body has been stubbornly attached for years.

Another way aerobic exercise can help is by lowering water retention that may be causing a weight-loss plateau. When the body loses fat, it tends to cling to fluid, driving up the numbers on the scale. Vigorous physical activity may help mobilize some of that fluid.

four

Getting Healthier

THERE IS STRONG EVIDENCE THAT THE RISK of several common diseases are significantly diminished in men and women who exercise on a regular basis. Even overweight and obese people who are active have more of a reduced risk of disease and premature death than people who are sedentary.

Despite these facts, regular exercise is elusive for most Americans. According to the July 1996 surgeon general's report on physical activity, more than 60 percent of adults in the United States don't exercise. Women are even less likely to be physically active than men, possibly because women are frequently left to balance work and family obligations and run out of time and energy for their own exercise needs.

These facts are hardly surprising when you consider how easy it is *not* to exercise. Technology supplies you with a growing array of computers and machines that do the physical work for you. Although you probably expend less energy today than your grandparents did a mere two generations ago, the mechanisms for regulating appetite and satiety have stayed the same.

Ironically, while technology and science have reduced your activity level, they also have allowed you to live longer, increasing the years that your body is subject to the effects of aging. This fact is reason enough to strive to live out those extra years feeling healthy and fit—and regular exercise can clearly help to that end.

Getting More Get-Up-and-Go

How can you exercise for energy when you don't have the energy to exercise in the first place? You don't have to run a marathon to get the energy-boosting benefits of physical activity and, by starting slowly and building up to more challenging workouts, you'll be able to eventually gain the stamina you need to help you feel more energetic for exercising and for everyday living.

- **Exercise makes energy.** Aerobic exercise—like walking, dancing, or biking—is important because it causes changes in the body's mitochondria. Mitochondria are microscopic "manufacturing plants" that are present in all our muscles and are responsible for turning stored fuel from food and oxygen into adenosine triphosphate, or ATP for short. ATP releases the charges of energy that allow our muscles to contract. Over time, exercise increases both the number of mitochondrion and their ability to churn out more ATP which, in turn, means you create more energy to fuel your muscles. This, along with a well-conditioned cardiovascular system's ability to feed your muscles with plenty of oxygen, is why exercise becomes easier as you keep doing it. It's also why you'll ultimately have more stamina for all your physical activities, whether it's cleaning the house or taking a bike ride.

- **Build strength, increase energy.** As you build muscle and get stronger, everyday activities require less of a percentage of your overall effort. Think of it as energy conservation. Now when you carry a suitcase or tote groceries it will be easier, and less tiring. Likewise when you engage in aerobic exercise. To some extent, stronger muscles make aerobic exercise less of a struggle and, ultimately, more enjoyable.

- **Don't worry, be happy.** Amidst all this talk about aerobic exercise and strength training, don't forget about enjoyment. If you enjoy your workouts, you'll be less likely to feel dragged down by stress and depression. If you are finding it hard to take pleasure in exercise, try enlisting a companion. Whether it is working out with a friend or even your dog, sometimes having company while you exercise makes all the difference.

HELPING YOU STAY WELL AND LIVE LONGER

Following are some of the ways physical activity works to protect your health and increase your longevity.

- **Improves cholesterol and triglyceride levels.** One of the ways exercise reduces the risk of heart disease is by causing weight loss, which in turns improves the levels of these fats (also called lipids) in the blood. (The "healthy range" you should be aiming for are cholesterol and triglyceride levels of 200 or lower, according to the National Cholesterol Education Program.) However, exercise also affects blood lipids independent of weight loss. It lowers levels of triglycerides and LDL (the "bad") cholesterol, which can create artery-clogging plaque and cause heart attack. It also raises the levels of HDL (the "good") cholesterol, the kind that clears plaque build up from the arteries.

  Although you can't change your lipid profile with a single exercise session, you'll see improvements as your body begins to adapt to activity. When you engage in regular aerobic exercise for a sustained period of time, the amount of oxygen you're able to take into your lungs—and, subsequently, the amount of oxygenated blood your heart is able to pump through your system—increase.

  Exercise also increases production of the enzyme lipoprotein lipase, which enables the muscles to use triglycerides for fuel. At the same time, the lipoprotein lipase causes LDL cholesterol to be eliminated by the body and bumps up the activity of protective HDL cholesterol.

- **Reduces blood pressure.** Hypertension—high blood pressure—is a risk factor for heart disease: People with a blood pressure over 160/95mm Hg have a 150 to 300 percent greater chance of heart failure and stroke. As you grow older, you're more likely to see a spike in your blood pressure level; however, like other factors associated with aging, hypertension may be more related to inactivity and increasing weight than to the passing years. Like other effects of aging, hypertension can also be remedied with exercise.

It's not completely clear how physical activity decreases blood pressure, though experts believe that it's related to exercise's dampening effect on the release of norepinephrine, a hormone that is controlled by the sympathetic nervous system. (It's the sympathetic nervous system that releases adrenaline and other hormones that get the body ready for "fight or flight" when danger is perceived.)

Aerobic exercise has been shown to not only lower blood pressure, but to do so fairly quickly—within three weeks to three months time. (Some preliminary evidence shows that strength training may also lower blood pressure.) Even if you don't have high blood pressure, regular exercise can help keep you from getting it: A study by the Cooper Institute of Aerobic Research found people who maintain their fitness over the years have a 34 percent lower risk of developing hypertension.

- **Burns abdominal fat.** Fat in the abdominal area is particularly troublesome because it is more easily mobilized into the bloodstream than other types of fat. The circulating fat can raise cholesterol levels as well as make the body more resistant to insulin, which, in turn, increases the risk of heart disease, high blood pressure, and diabetes.

  The good news is that exercise burns abdominal fat preferentially over fat in other areas of the body. A nationwide study done in Great Britain, called the Allied Dunbar National Fitness Survey, found that women who took regular brisk walks had proportionately smaller waistlines than sedentary women of the same weight. Some research also suggests that strength training, not just calorie-burning aerobic exercise, can spur the body to turn to abdominal fat for fuel.

- **Improves insulin sensitivity.** Insulin is a hormone secreted by the pancreas that is responsible for moving glucose—a form of sugar derived from carbohydrates—into the muscle cells, where it's then used for energy. When the cells become resistant to insulin, glucose builds up in the bloodstream and wreaks all kinds of havoc, ultimately setting the stage for type 2 diabetes.

By lowering body fat, physical activity increases the body's sensitivity to insulin, so that smaller amounts of insulin are required to usher glucose into the muscle cells. But exercise also improves insulin sensitivity independently of weight loss: Working muscles have a much greater capacity to clear glucose from the bloodstream than idle muscles. In addition, while it's long been known that aerobic exercise lowers the chances of developing diabetes, recent research suggests that strength training may also improve insulin sensitivity.

• **Stops bone loss.** The duo of adequate calcium intake and exercise is one of the best tools you have for maintaining bone. Exercise saves bone because bone responds to increased stress. When you place a load on a bone by doing what's referred to as weight-bearing exercise, such as walking or aerobic dancing, it stimulates the bone cells to create a buildup of calcium, fortifying themselves against depletion. (Of course, this effect is predicated on adequate calcium intake.) But remember that all your muscles need exercise to prevent overall bone loss: for example, running prevents bone loss in the legs, tennis improves bone density in the arm (unfortunately, only one of them—unless you're ambidextrous), and so on.

Early evidence suggests that weight training may also prevent bone loss. In a study conducted at the USDA's Jean Mayer Human Nutrition Research Center at Tufts University, researchers divided 39 women, ages 50 to 70, into two groups. One group exercised twice a week for 45 minutes on weight machines. The other women did no exercise. After one year, the strength trainers had stronger bones as well as more muscle and improved balance, all of which decreased their risks of falling and breaking a bone.

Unfortunately, the bone-preserving effect of exercise doesn't appear to be strong enough to completely prevent the accelerated bone loss that occurs during menopause.

Assessing the Family Factor

Does having a family history of disease increase the likelihood that you have inherited a predisposition to certain conditions? Yes and no. It may simply mean that you have to take even greater precautions than someone who doesn't have a genetic history of illness. Genetics researchers believe that heredity is only partially responsible for increasing a person's susceptibility to disease and that lifestyle can have a large impact.

If you have a family history of disease, it's a good idea to discuss your risks with your physician. Maintaining a healthy weight, watching your diet, and exercising are preventive measures for just about every kind of malady, but your doctor can clue you into any additional steps you should be taking. To give you an idea of whether your family history warrants a discussion of your risks, here's what is known about the genetic influences of the more common diseases.

- **Heart Disease.** If your father, grandfather, or brother had a heart attack before age 55, or a mother, grandmother, or sister had one before age 65, you have a higher risk of having one yourself. This is especially true if you are African-American, since African-Americans have a higher risk of heart disease than Caucasians and suffer a more severe form of the disease. You also have a 50 percent higher risk of sudden cardiac arrest if a parent has suffered a heart attack or cardiac arrest and a 70 percent higher risk if a sibling has. (Cardiac arrest occurs when the heart stops beating due to

However, physical activity can have some protective effect, especially when combined with hormone replacement therapy and, of course, adequate calcium intake.

- **Lowers the risk of some cancers.** Although the relationship between exercise and cancer still isn't completely clear, epidemiological studies show that physical activity seems to offer protections against some forms of the disease.

The connection between breast cancer and exercise was first brought to light by a now-famous Harvard University study published in 1985. Researcher Rose Frisch and her colleagues found that women who had been college athletes an abnormal heart beat. Heart attack occurs when the arteries are blocked.)

- **Cancer.** Only about 5 to 10 percent of most types of cancer are due to genetic defects passed on through families. Having relatives on the maternal side of your family who've had breast cancer, increases your rate but, again, only about 5 to 10 percent. The family risk of colon cancer is slightly higher: Your risk is 10 to 15 percent above that of someone without a family history if a close family member has had the disease.

- **Diabetes.** If you have a parent with insulin-dependent diabetes (type 1), you have about a 4 to 6 percent chance of getting it yourself. If you have a parent with non-insulin-dependent diabetes (type 2), you have a 7 to 14 percent risk. African-Americans, Mexican Americans, and Pima Indians have an even higher risk.

- **Osteoporosis.** Researchers have not yet been able to quantify the impact of heredity on osteoporosis. Although there are many factors that contribute to the risk of disease, it's largely believed that having a family history on the maternal side—grandmother, mother, sister—increases your risk of brittle bones. This may be because members of the same family tend to reach the same level of peak bone mass. Thus, if your mother didn't lay down a healthy amount of bone in her teens and twenties, it's likely that you may have followed suit.

had a lower incidence of breast cancer as well as cancers of the reproductive system (ovaries, cervix, vagina, and uterus) than women who were nonathletes. Following up with a new study in 1989, the researchers found that athletic women were also less likely to get other types of cancer, including lung, thyroid, bladder, lymphoma, and Hodgkin's disease.

Physical activity most likely offers protection by influencing the levels of hormones and various metabolic processes that are associated with certain cancers. Exercise, for instance, is known to have an effect on levels of estrogen, a hormone that contributes to breast and ovarian cancers. It also enhances the immune system, possibly inhibiting cancer cell formation, and may help prevent colon cancer by increasing the speed at which waste goes through the intestine, limiting the colon's contact with potential carcinogens.

- **Eases joint pain.** Simply keeping the joints moving may prevent them from becoming stiff. Studies show that exercise lessens joint pain, and may even help ward off discomfort in the first place.

   In addition, all exercise helps keep the bones and cartilage, which make up the joints healthy, while strengthening the ligaments and muscles so that they're better able to protect and stabilize the joints. Flexibility exercises, in particular, can help decrease stiffness and increase range of motion. Weight training and aerobic exercise—by strengthening the muscles and increasing circulation respectively—are integral to easing and preventing arthritis as well.

THE BODY-MIND CONNECTION

The mind sometimes seems entirely separate from the body, but in fact, the two are inextricably linked. It makes sense, then, that physical activity influences not only what's going on below the neck, but what's going on above it, too. Here, a look at how exercise works to improve your mood.

- **Less stress, less weight.** Part of exercise's mind-body link can be traced to the fact that it's one of the most effective ways to relieve stress. Stress is not only known to take a toll on health, but to cause weight gain, too, since many people turn to food in times of chaos or crisis.

   Exercise can also help you overcome stress-induced overeating by making you feel calmer. This may be particularly true of aerobic workouts, which leave many exercisers with the feel-good effect, known as "runner's high," thanks to the neurotransmitters in the brain called beta-endorphins. Endorphins are a by-product of activity in the nervous system. As vigorous movement heats up the body, the sympathetic nervous system—the part of the nervous system that responds to stress—releases epinephrine (otherwise known as adrenaline). But because it takes too much energy to stay perched in this hyperaware state for long, countermeasures occur: To calm the body back down, opiate-like beta-endorphins are dispatched from the pituitary gland to receptor sites in the brain. Most likely, this chain of events results in improved spirits and reduced tension and anxiety.

Some researchers also believe that exercise may increase the brain's emission of alpha waves, which are associated with a relaxed mental state. For many, though, a good workout may just function as a good time-out, an interval during which the day's stresses and strains can be forgotten.

- **Exercising against illness**. Physical activity may indirectly help lower the risk of illness because it buffers the effects of stress and depression. For instance, when researchers at the University of Washington looked at the relationship between stress and visits to the university health center, they found that the students who had the greatest amount of stress also had the greatest number of visits to the center. While this fact was not surprising, another one was: Those students who were stressed out, but also engaged in regular aerobic exercise, had fewer visits to the health center than their less-fit, highly-stressed peers.

- **Improved body image and self-esteem.** Losing weight can bolster your self-esteem and confidence. But losing weight using exercise—or even just becoming more fit without dropping scads of pounds—may by especially helpful when it comes to seeing yourself in a better light. Too often women think of their bodies only in terms of how *fashionable* (that is, how thin) they are. Physical activity gives you the chance to think about how *functional* your body is. When you exercise, you accomplish physical feats that aren't easy; every walk you take and pound you lift should

Exercise and the Common Cold

Can working out help you avoid a case of the sniffles? The answer is, for the most part, yes. Moderate exercise actually boosts immune function. However, exhaustive exercise, associated with marathons and elite triathlons, can increase your risk of getting sick.

Some of the pioneering work on exercise and immunity has been done by David Neiman, a researcher at Appalachian State University in Boone, North Carolina. One of Neiman's most notable studies involved putting a group of sedentary women on a walking regimen and comparing their rates of illness with those of women in a non-exercising group. During a 15-week period coinciding with flu season, the walkers averaged five sick days per person while the inactive group averaged 11 days.

The exercisers' lower rates of illness can most likely be attributed to an increase in natural killer cell activity that has been observed with moderate exercise. Exercise also increases circulation, which enhances the ability of these virus-disabling cells to move around the body and catch up with foreign invaders. Another plus: Regular physical activity may blunt the decrease in T-cell function (T-cells defend against infections, too) that often accompanies age.

For most people, physical activity is an immune booster. As long as you keep your workouts at a healthy level—that is, to the point where they don't cause you to become extremely fatigued or to suffer symptoms of overtraining such as cessation or irregularity of your periods, insomnia, injuries, an elevated pulse rate, or irritability—your resistance to disease should go up, not down.

remind you that your body is an amazing machine. Evidence suggests that it will.

In a study conducted at Brigham Young University in Utah, researchers found that participating in either a walking or a strength-training program for 12 weeks improved the body image of 60 previously sedentary women between the ages of 35 and 49.

Interestingly, the women who had the most improvement in body image were the women who strength trained than performed the aerobic workouts. This may be true because improvement in strength training is more noticeable—

as you get better, you're able to increase the amount of weight you can lift. It also may have bolstered their body images because it brings about changes in muscle tone fairly quickly.

- **Keeping a mental edge.** While older adults' minds may not be as alert and their memories may not be as sharp as those of younger adults, there is evidence that mental ability doesn't have to decline as we age, and exercise can play a role in keeping it in shape. One study, for instance, showed that men ages 50 to 62 years old who exercised for four months processed information more quickly than their sedentary peers. The reason, the researchers postulated, may be that exercise increases the amount of oxygen delivered to the brain.

  The types of exercise that require learning skills, such as tennis or soccer, may help keep the mind fit as well. Anything that calls for mental, along with physical, exercise generates new brain synapses, improving the connections between the neurons and helping the brain think quicker.

  Some evidence also suggests that exercise can help promote the growth of new brain cells. In 1984, a group of scientists from various fields embarked upon a project known as the MacArthur Foundation Study on Successful Aging. One of the study's findings suggested that an increase in physical activity in adult rats corresponded with an increase in a substance called nerve growth factor, which promotes the creation of brain cells related to memory. If the same effect takes place in humans, which the researchers suspect it does, it indicates that exercise enhances memory function.

Part II

INGREDIENTS FOR SUCCESS

five

Exercising to Lose Weight and Fight Aging

IN ORDER TO LOSE WEIGHT, you must burn more calories than you take in.

You'll also want your exercise program to be challenging enough to improve your cardiovascular system (including heart, lungs, and blood vessels) and to help you maintain muscle mass and bone density. Put together, all these components sound like a large fitness package. But if you truly want to fight the effects of aging and burn calories, not only while you're in motion, but when you're at rest, too, you have to (at some stage) incorporate all these components into your fitness regimen.

Yet don't assume that you have to take on all three elements at once. For example, as you embark on the **Fit Factor Plan** (the exercises begin in chapter 7), first focus on the ten-step routine using weights. As you grow stronger and more confident, you may want to include a leisurely (or more structured) walk, run, or bike ride into the equation. The key is to break the total fitness picture down into easy-to-accomplish pieces. Otherwise, if you take on too much too soon you may find yourself giving up before you even really got started.

Profile in Fitness

NAME: AUDREY K.

OCCUPATION: ELEMENTARY ART TEACHER

HOME STATE: WISCONSIN

AGE: 46 YEARS OLD

BEFORE WEIGHT: 221 LBS

AFTER WEIGHT: 149 LBS

HEIGHT: 5'8"

HOW SHE STAYS STRONG AND FIT:

WALKING, 20 MINUTES PER DAY

CYCLING, 10–15 MILES, 3–4 TIMES PER WEEK

*"I have a better appreciation of what my body
is capable of doing. It empowers me, and touches
every part of my life."*

I'd always been heavy and it gradually got worse as I got older. I tried many weight-loss programs including Weight Watchers, where I lost about 60 pounds on the Program. But then I stopped going to the meetings, journaling, and exercising, and quickly regained the weight.

I always hated working out; I was a very inactive person. Once I made the commitment to myself to go back on the Program, I vowed I would follow it just as it was prescribed—including 20 minutes of daily exercise. I thought, "I can do that. It's only 20 minutes."

But I hated every second of it. Physically, I was very out of shape. It took everything I had to keep going to the meetings and exercising. I live in the country, so I walked a lot. In the winter, I'd walk in the gym after school just for the requisite 20 minutes. I still hated the exercise.

Gradually, as I saw the weight coming off and my body toning up—and I began feeling stronger—I realized I wanted to exercise more, that I really liked doing it. Now, I actually enjoy it—something I never thought I'd say.

When I reached my goal weight, I treated myself to a bicycle. I hadn't ridden one since high school! Now, I'll try to ride between 10 and 15 miles, three to four times a week. I feel healthier and stronger, and I have more energy. It's changed my whole perception about my wellbeing. I have a better appreciation of what my body is capable of doing. It empowers me, and touches every part of my life.

GET READY, GET SET

To get you ready for your fitness plan, consider the following guidelines, based on the work of the American College of Sports Medicine (ACSM), an organization with members in the medical, scientific, and education communities. These guidelines can be applied to the **Fit Factor Plan**; if you are starting your own routine, you can use them as well. Here's what you need to do to drop pounds, halt aging, and improve your overall health.

1. The Strength-Training Component

The objective of strength training is to increase the load on the muscles, which then attempt to overcome or resist that load (the reason strength training is also referred to as resistance training). When challenged this way, the muscles adapt by thickening existing muscle fibers and making a number of other adjustments that ultimately increase your muscle mass and strength.

There are several options for building strength, but weight lifting is the most effective. However, it isn't always easy or convenient to work all of the muscle groups with weights; calisthenics or basic exercises like push-ups and sit-ups can remedy these problems. Calisthenics are effective because they allow you to use the weight of your own body to load the muscles. But remember: Since calisthenics don't readily allow you to incrementally increase the load you place on a muscle, their effects are limited.

While strength training doesn't burn a considerable amount of calories, it does lead to changes in the structure of your muscles, which eventually makes your body a better overall calorie burner.

The Prescription: Strength training is a very site-specific form of exercise, that is, it only affects the area you are working. For example, biceps curls with hand weights build the biceps and forearm muscles; push-ups build the arms, chest, and shoulders; and so on. For this reason, it's important that your strength-training program cover all the major muscle groups: arms (biceps and triceps), shoulders (deltoids), chest (pectoral muscles), abdomen (external obliques and rectus abdominis), back (latissimus dorsi and trapezius), hips (glutei), and legs (quadriceps and hamstrings).

Surprisingly, a regimen that targets all body areas doesn't require a lot of time. A comprehensive strength-training workout can generally be performed within a half-hour. Another great thing about strength training is that you can quickly see how you're progressing. Each time you increase the amount of weight you're lifting or add a few more repetitions, you get instant evidence that you're growing stronger.

How Often: Two to three days a week. Even if you're starting at a very low level of fitness, you should strength train at least two days a week. The muscles have to be worked more than just occasionally—although they shouldn't be worked consecutive days, since muscles need recovery time in order to be able to adapt to the stress you place upon them.

How Much: One set of 8 to 12 repetitions per exercise. Both weight lifting and calisthenics are traditionally done in sets, or a number of repetitions. In the past, it was thought that you needed to do at least two sets of each weight lifting exercise to affect change in the muscles. But recent studies have shown that one set of 8 to 12 repetitions offers nearly as much improvement as two sets.

Equally as important as the number of sets and repetitions is the amount of weight you're lifting. How much you lift during each exercise should be enough to cause your muscles to fatigue considerably toward the last repetitions in a set. In other words, if you're doing 8 to 12 repetitions, the last two should feel so difficult that you can barely complete them.

2. The Aerobic Component

Aerobic exercise boosts your heart rate for a sustained period of time. During aerobic exercise, your body is fueled primarily by oxygen in combination with warehoused energy (such as carbohydrates in the form of glycogen and fat from your fat stores). Walking, running, swimming, cycling, aerobic dancing, inline skating, jumping rope, rowing, and cross-country skiing are all examples of aerobic exercise.

You also may have heard of anaerobic exercise, a type of exercise that is performed without the aid of adequate oxygen to the muscles. Without oxygen, your body is only capable of producing a small amount of energy—the reason you can only perform an anaerobic activity like sprinting for a short period of time.

The Prescription: When it comes to aerobic exercise, the rules are simple: The benefits you reap from physical activity depend on how often and how long you perform each session, and whether or not you fall within your target heart rate. Here are some specifics about the frequency, intensity and duration of aerobic exercise.

How Hard: Ideally, aerobic workouts are in the 65 to 80 percent range of your maximum heart rate. Exercise physiologists judge the intensity of exercise by how it affects your heart rate or, more specifically, how close it gets you to your maximum heart rate. Your maximum heart rate (MHR) is the number of times your heart beats when you are exercising at top capacity. In order to cause the physiological adaptations mentioned above and to burn an adequate number of calories, you'll need to work out at a pace that is anywhere from 55 to 90 percent of your MHR, or your target heart rate (THR). (If extremely unfit, start at 55 percent; see box below to determine your range.)

How Often: Three to five days a week. No matter how sedentary you've been, you'll want to start exercising at least three times a week. Unless you've been exercising regularly, your initial workouts will probably be fairly short in duration and low intensity. If this is the case, the only way you'll really be able to burn a substantial number of calories is to exercise more often. As you get fitter and you exercise for longer periods of time, you won't have to exercise as frequently.

In the beginning, you'll want to exercise at the low end of your THR, but even as your fitness improves, your workout should never leave you gasping for breath. You should still be able to carry on a

How Hard Are You Working?

As you engage in aerobic exercise, your goal should be to spend the majority of your time at your target heart rate, the optimal number of beats per minute. Ideally, you want to work out at a THR that's between 65 and 80 percent of your maximum heart rate (MHR), but if you've been fairly inactive, you may want to start out at 55 percent of your MHR. Here's how to figure out the number—actually a range of numbers—you'll want to shoot for.

DO THE MATH

Maximum heart rate = 220 – your age in years
Target heart rate = 65 to 80 percent of your MHR

The THR of a 40-year-old starting at a slow pace:
$220 - 40 = 180$
$.55 \times 180 = 99$ beats per minute
$.65 \times 180 = 117$ beats per minute
THR range: 99 to 117 beats per minute

The THR of a 40-year-old starting at a moderate pace:
$220 - 40 = 180$
$.65 \times 180 = 117$ beats per minute
$.80 \times 180 = 144$ beats per minute
THR range: 117 to 144 beats per minute

TAKE YOUR PULSE

Once you've determined your THR, you'll need to see if you're meeting your goals while exercising. Wear a watch or have a clock handy. In the middle of your workout, slow down (but try not to stop) and quickly take your pulse. Do so by placing the index and middle finger of one hand on the inside of the wrist of your other hand. If you can't feel your pulse that way, place the same two fingers very lightly under and to the left side of your chin, right in the crook of your neck and head. (This is your carotid artery so be careful not to press too hard.) Count your pulse for 15 seconds, starting at zero, then multiply the number you get by four to determine beats per minute. Compare your pulse rate to your THR. If you're under, try to work a little harder. If you're over, slow down.

conversation as you're working out. A few general points to keep in mind:

- The longer you can keep going, the better.

- If you're working too hard, you won't be able to sustain the activity for burning calories.

- Don't be discouraged. People getting fit can still achieve a significant training effect at a low intensity.

How Long: 20 to 60 minutes of continuous exercise with a minimum calorie burn of 250 to 300 calories per session. The minimum amount of continuous activity recommended for improving aerobic capacity is 20 minutes, but remember: There is a definite correlation between the length of an exercise session, the number of calories burned, and the level of cardiovascular fitness achieved. Also, consider that you can break up your workouts into ten-minute bouts and still get tangible benefits.

The duration of your workout may also be influenced by the intensity of your exercise. For instance, if you exercise at a low intensity for a fairly long time, you can burn the same amount of calories as you would if you exercised at a higher intensity for a shorter period. When weight loss is your goal, you should aim for a balance of intensity/duration that allows you to burn 250 to 300 calories per session at least three days a week (or, as an alternative, a balance that allows you to burn 200 calories four days a week).

3. The Flexibility Component

The physiological changes you'll experience as a result of flexibility exercises aren't as dramatic as those you get from strength training and aerobic workouts, but they're an important adjunct to a well-rounded program. As the body ages, the muscles tighten up, not only making exercise more difficult to perform, but also increasing your chance of injury. Flexibility exercises, or stretches, improve the joints' range of motion and enable the muscles to have more "give," lowering the risk of strains and sprains.

Can You Get By With Short Bouts of Exercise?

Since it may be easier for some people to sneak in ten minutes of exercise here and there rather than setting aside a whole block of time, researchers have been examining the effects of short bouts of exercise.

In one of the most recent studies, conducted at the University of Pittsburgh School of Medicine, 28 exercisers followed a program of long bouts of exercise and 28 followed a short-bout (10-minute each) program. Both groups worked out five days a week, progressing from 20 to 40 minutes of exercise over a period of 20 weeks. At the end of the study, both groups had similar increases in aerobic capacity, but those exercisers who worked out in short bouts proved to adhere to their fitness regime more avidly and ended up putting in more workout time than the long-bout exercisers. They also lost slightly more weight.

Depending on your schedule, splitting up your workout may in fact work better for you. But one caveat: If it's your goal to get fit enough to do something that requires endurance, short sessions won't train you properly. If, say, you want to run or walk a 10-K race, cycle 25 miles on a weekend, or just be able to swim for a half-hour straight, you'll need to work up to doing these distances in one fell swoop. Short bouts of exercise will indeed make you more fit, help you lose weight, and improve your health, but long bouts will more effectively allow you to accomplish the same while helping you acquire more stamina for the specific exercise performance goal you may wish to accomplish.

The Prescription: Like strength training, stretching is site specific: The muscles you stretch will reap the benefit so, as with strength training, you need to have a well-rounded program. The safest type of stretches are known as static stretches and require slowly moving into a position and holding (without bouncing) the stretch for 20 to 30 seconds.

How Often: Complete a full range of stretching exercises after each workout session. Stretching exercises should be performed at least two to three times a week, but your best bet is to follow each exercise session (strength training or aerobic) with a few minutes of stretching.

ROUTINE VERSUS FORMAL EXERCISE

By following all three of the exercise prescriptions, you will boost your weight loss, fight aging, and improve muscular strength and cardiovascular fitness—and lower your risk of disease. But you should be aware that you also can improve your health and slim down with less formal exercise. In fact, simply making sure you move a lot throughout your day—whether it be sweeping the floor or walking to your destination—can lower your risk of premature death.

One of the landmark studies that looked at the role of routine activities (also called lifestyle activities) on health was performed at the Cooper Institute for Aerobics Research. The researchers placed half of a group of 235 sedentary and slightly overweight men and women on a six-month, structured, intensive exercise program. The

The Energy Expenditure of Everyday Activities

These calorie-burn counts are for a 150-pound woman. If you're heavier, you'll burn slightly more; if you're lighter, you'll burn slightly less.

ACTIVITY	CALORIES BURNED/HOUR
Car washing	288
House cleaning	252
Cooking	186
Grocery shopping	252
Digging in the garden	516
Mowing the lawn	456
Raking	222
Mopping floors	252
Scrubbing floors	444
Washing windows	276
Vacuuming	264
Sitting around	84

other half were placed on a program involving routine lifestyle activities, like walking instead of riding and taking stairs instead of elevators. After six months, the participants were asked to continue the exercise for another 18 months. At the end of two years, both groups had significant—and about the same—improvements in heart function and blood pressure. Neither group lost weight, but they both reduced their percentage of body fat, which means that they increased their lean body mass. What's more, a quarter of the participants maintained a 10 percent improvement in cardiovascular fitness, which the researchers translated into a 15 percent reduction in mortality.

Another important study, conducted at Johns Hopkins University School of Medicine, found that routine activities may even help you slim down. Enlisting 40 obese individuals who were placed in two groups, one group followed a structured aerobic exercise program, while the other engaged only in lifestyle activities of moderate intensity. Both groups followed a low-fat diet. After 16 weeks, the aerobic exercise group had lost an average of 18 pounds and the lifestyle group had lost about 17. Both groups also reduced their triglyceride and cholesterol levels significantly. When the researchers followed up a year later, the aerobic exercise group had regained nearly four pounds, while the lifestyle exercisers had put back on a mere two pounds.

So, if all you need to do to stay healthy and lose weight is walk your dog, rake leaves, wash your car, or polish furniture, why bother following a more formalized exercise plan? As much as these lifestyle activities can benefit your overall health, they don't do as good a job of substantially increasing your stamina, helping you lose weight, or deflecting the effects of aging as formalized exercise does. Routine exercise may improve your health, but formal exercise makes you more fit, maximizes your calorie burning, aids in weight loss, and lowers your risk of disease even more.

Also, a well-rounded, formal exercise program may be more effective for maintaining muscle and bone. For instance, the women in the Johns Hopkins study who did aerobic exercise lost considerably less lean body mass (muscle and bone) than the women who did lifestyle exercise.

An Alternative Way to Determine Your Intensity

The best tool you have for determining how hard you're working is the target heart rate equation. If you're loathe to solve even the simplest math problem, this is your next best option: The Borg Rating of Perceived Exertion (RPE) scale, which allows you to measure intensity by how you feel. Each number on the scale corresponds to a percentage of maximum heart rate, but you don't need to do any calculations to figure it out. Just check in with yourself mid-workout. Your threshold for cardiovascular-aerobic training falls just about at an exercise level that you would rate as "somewhat hard".

RPE SCALE

6	
7	very, very light
8	
9	very light
10	
11	fairly light
12	
13	somewhat hard
14	(equivalent of 70% of maximum heart rate)
15	hard
16	
17	very hard
18	
19	very, very hard

These studies drive home an important point: Formal exercise and lifestyle exercise don't have to—and shouldn't—be mutually exclusive. The best way to lose weight and keep it off is to follow a formal strength training/aerobic/flexibility plan *and* stay active with everyday activities. When a National Institutes of Health panel on physical activity and cardiovascular health recently convened, they recommended that Americans try to accumulate 30 minutes of moderate-intensity physical activity every day of the week.

The bottom line? Don't rest on your laurels just because you're doing formal exercise on certain days of the week. On those days when you're not doing your regular workout—and even on your workout days—keep moving. All those extra calories burned will add up to help you drop pounds and keep them off. And you'll be doing the utmost to keep yourself fit, healthy, and energetic.

six

Testing Yourself

MOST LIKELY, YOU FALL INTO ONE OF TWO exercise categories: You've glanced at the exercises on the coming pages and are ready to jump right in, or you're clueless about whether or not you should even begin. In either case, it's a good idea to bone up on some fitness basics—including how to fit working out into your schedule, and how quickly you should expect to progress—before embarking upon an exercise program. (Check with your doctor or health care provider before starting any exercise regimen.)

If you're revved up to begin working out, you're on the right track. But remember: Starting an exercise program in too high a gear also can cause rapid burnout. Ease into your regime and try different routines to find what works best for you. On the other hand, if you're reticent and unmotivated, understanding the best way to plan for exercise will help you get off to a strong start.

Here are four fundamental steps to prepare yourself before you begin the **Fit Factor Plan.**

#1: DETERMINE YOUR STARTING POINT

One of the basic tenets of getting in shape is that you shouldn't compare your fitness level to anyone else's. Some people, for instance, are innately flexible in the hips and hamstrings while others have more upper body flexibility. Certain individuals are genetically predisposed to have more muscle, while some may have a naturally high aerobic capacity. What matters is not where you stand in relation to others, but where you're starting—and where you're going.

In light of this, the following fitness tests are not designed to tell you if you're in good or bad shape, but to act as a benchmark so that you can see how far you progress. As you begin to exercise regularly, you will most certainly make some headway. These numbers will let you see just how much.

Test your upper body strength

You'll need a sturdy chair; brace it against a wall so that it won't move when you do.

1. Sit on the edge of the chair with your legs straight out in front of you and your heels on the floor.

2. Place your hands on the front edge of the chair and move your hips forward until they're off the seat. Your arms should be almost straight.

3. Lower your hips slowly toward the floor until your elbows are bent at right angles. Then, press your body upward until your arms are almost straight. Take four seconds to lower, then two seconds to raise yourself back up.

4. Perform as many consecutive chair dips as you can before experiencing discomfort or burning; don't move faster or slower than six seconds per repetition.

5. Record your result, then retest yourself after a month.

Test your lower-body strength

You'll need a sturdy chair.

1. Stand with your feet shoulder-width apart and heels on the floor, 6 to 12 inches in front of a chair (your back is to the chair).

2. Cross your arms and, keeping your back as straight as possible (look straight ahead with your eyes fixed on a spot on

the wall), squat down until your buttocks lightly touches the chair seat. Take four seconds to go down and two seconds to raise back up. (Do not go lower than chair height to lessen the strain on your knees.)

3. Do as many of these half-squats as you can without bouncing, feeling extreme pain, or losing your balance.

4. Record your result, then retest yourself after a month.

Test your aerobic ability

You'll need a premeasured distance of one flat mile and a watch with a second hand or stopwatch.

1. Walk for three to five minutes to warm up, then stretch gently.

2. Note the time on your watch or start the stopwatch and begin walking along the mile course as quickly as you can but at a pace that you can maintain for the entire mile.

3. Note the time it took you to complete the mile. Cool down and stretch again.

4. Record your time, then retest yourself after a month.

Test your upper-body flexibility

You'll need a friend, a felt pen, a full-length mirror, and enough space to stretch out.

1. Do some light, "big muscle" calisthenic movements (e.g. arm circles, side bends) for several minutes to warm up before you measure flexibility.

2. Stand sideways in front of the mirror.

3. Reach your hands behind your buttocks and clasp them together, palms touching.

4. Raise your hands as high as possible without leaning forward so that your arms are flush with the mirror.

5. Have your friend mark on the mirror how high your hands reach up.

6. Record the number of inches from the bottom of the mirror. Repeat two more times.

7. Record your best score to determine your flexibility level. Retest yourself in a month.

Test your lower-body flexibility

You'll need a yardstick, tape, and an open space.

1. Do some light, "big muscle" calisthenic movements (e.g. arm circles, side bends) for several minutes to warm up before you measure flexibility.

2. Sit on the floor so that your feet are about 12 inches apart, legs straight.

3. Lay a yardstick on the floor lengthwise between your legs so that the beginning is even with your knees; tape the yardstick down to secure it.

4. Place one hand on top of the other and reach as far forward between your legs as comfortably possible. Don't overextend.

5. Note how far on the yardstick you've reached. Repeat two more times.

6. Record your best score to determine your flexibility level. Then retest yourself in a month.

#2: MAKE THE TIME

When is the best time to exercise? The answer to that question is another question: When do you *have* time to exercise? The hour of the day that you should slot exercise into your schedule is the hour when you are most likely to adhere to your plan. If you always work late or are too tired by the end of the day to work out, don't schedule evening workouts. Likewise, if you find it difficult to roll out of bed and into your exercise clothes in the morning, try a time later in the day.

Interestingly, some research shows that people who engage in physical activity in the morning are actually more likely to stick with it than evening exercisers (possibly because leaving exercise until later in the day creates a greater chance of getting waylaid by other responsibilities).

Another point you might want to consider is that you should move when exercise *feels* best. According to studies conducted at Liverpool John Moores University in England, the body is best primed for physical activity from 5 PM to 7 PM. In the late afternoon and early evening, the lungs literally breathe easier because their airways are more open. Physical strength is also highest at 6 PM, and since body temperature is higher later in the day, the muscles and joints are more flexible.

There are 101 ways to schedule your workouts, but we've supplied the following schedules to give you examples of what works for people with various time constraints. They are also based on the ideal number of workouts you should be working toward per week: three strength-training sessions; six aerobic sessions; and flexibility exercises following each single or combined workout.

One point you may notice is that on some sample days, the strength training sessions immediately follow the aerobic sessions. The two sessions are combined because cardiovascular exercise is an excellent way to warm up your muscles for strength training, reducing your risk of injury. But it's not essential that you do the two together. If your time allowance per session is short, do them separately. Also, if you're a beginner who feels exhausted after the aerobic segments of your workouts, leave the weight workouts until later.

In addition, we've included an "active day off." On the days you give yourself a break from formal exercise, try to stay active, walking and taking stairs when you can or doing physically demanding work around the house.

#3: EXPECT A *REASONABLE* PROGRESSION

Just as each person possesses individual physical assets, everyone also gets in shape at a different rate. A person actually has a

WHEN NIGHTTIME IS THE RIGHT TIME		
Monday	6 PM:	• Walking outdoors (summer) or on a treadmill (winter) • Stretches
Tuesday	6 PM:	• Step aerobics tape • Strength training • Stretches
Wednesday	6 PM:	• Walking outdoors (summer) or on a treadmill (winter) • Stretches
Thursday	6 PM:	• Walking outdoors (summer) or on a treadmill (winter) • Strength training • Stretches
Friday	Active day off	
Saturday	4 PM:	• Aerobics class • Strength training • Stretches
Sunday	4 PM:	• Walking outdoors • Stretches

genetically-determined "pretraining status" that governs his or her capacity to adapt to exercise—so don't get discouraged if the woman working out on the stair climber next to you begins to look lean and trim.

During the first few weeks of The Plan, you'll have the most success if you focus on the immediate benefits of your workouts. You probably won't lose weight or see muscle definition overnight, but you will probably feel more energetic immediately. Focus on how good you feel after working up a sweat and give yourself credit for changing your life. The other benefits—increased strength, shapelier muscles, reduced body fat, and an improved cardiovascular system—will follow.

FOR THE MORNING PERSON		
Monday	7 AM:	• Swimming laps
	6 PM:	• Strength training
		• Stretches
Tuesday	7 AM:	• Walking outdoors
		• Stretches
Wednesday	7 AM:	• Swimming laps
	6 PM:	• Strength training
		• Stretches
Thursday	7 AM:	• Walking outdoors
		• Stretches
Friday	7 AM:	• Strength training
		• Stretches
Saturday	9 AM:	• Yoga class
Sunday	Active day off	

A LUNCH-TIME ROUTINE		
Monday	12 PM:	• Walking
		• Stretches
Tuesday	12 PM:	• Strength training
		• Stretches
Wednesday	12 PM:	• Stationary cycling
		• Stretches
Thursday	12 PM:	• Strength training
		• Stretches
Friday	Active day off	
Saturday	9 AM:	• Walking
		• Strength training
		• Stretches
Sunday	12 PM:	• Bike riding
		• Stretches

A CATCH-AS-CAN REGIME		
Monday	7 AM:	• 20 mins Treadmill walking
		• Stretches
	6 PM:	• 20 mins Aerobics video
		• Stretches
Tuesday	7 AM:	• 15 mins Upper body strength training
		• Upper body stretches
	6 PM:	• 15 mins Lower body strength training
		• Lower body stretches
Wednesday	7 AM:	• 20 mins Treadmill walking
		• Stretches
	12 PM:	• 20 mins Walking outdoors
		• Stretches
Thursday	7 AM:	• 15 mins Upper body strength training
		• Upper body stretches
	6 PM:	• 15 mins Lower body strength training
		• Lower body stretches
Friday	7 AM:	• 20 mins Treadmill walking
		• Stretches
	6 PM:	• 20 mins Aerobics video
		• Stretches
Saturday	9 AM:	•1 hr Aerobics video
		• Strength training
		• Stretches
Sunday		Active day off

When? Here is a general estimate of how long it takes to start seeing results.

- **To lose weight.** How much weight you lose during the coming weeks depends on how many calories you consume *and* how many calories you burn, per week. If you're following

Weight Watchers **1•2•3 Success Plan** and exercising to burn 250 to 300 calories five times a week, you should begin to see results in four to eight weeks. Be advised, though, that you may not see as big a loss on the scale as you might expect, since you'll probably be gaining some muscle (which weighs more than fat). Still, don't let the numbers discourage you. Since muscle occupies less space (it's more dense) than an equivalent amount of fat, your clothes will probably fit more loosely than before, evidence that you are indeed reshaping your body.

- **To build calorie-hungry muscle.** Due to changes in the nerves that control your muscles, you should begin to see an increase in your strength by week four of your work-outs—though it might take a little longer before you actually begin to build muscle. Expect to *see* noticeable changes in muscle tone in eight to ten weeks—but you will *feel* noticeable effects within several weeks.

- **To increase your aerobic capacity.** The more sedentary you've been, the quicker you will improve your aerobic capacity (although your improvements will eventually level off). If you engage in cardiovascular exercise five times a week, you should be able to increase your aerobic capacity 10 to 20 percent in about ten weeks.

- **To improve flexibility.** Small changes in your muscles' elasticity should be noticeable right away. Even as you hold a stretch, you will see that your muscles gradually loosen up. Expect to see real improvements in about four to eight weeks.

#4: START WITH THE RIGHT MIND-SET

Rigorous as it can be, the physical, rather than psychological, aspects of exercise are often easier to grapple with. Maintaining motivation and enthusiasm are the toughest challenges you'll face in the weeks to come. Before you dive into the Fit Factor Plan, take a couple of steps that will help you mentally prepare for the task.

- **Forget about gym class.** You're about to embark upon a program that will bring out your physical prowess. It is not about becoming a soccer whiz or developing a killer backhand, it's about getting stronger. No matter how good or bad you were at sports in the past, many activities—including strength training—don't require a lot of skill or coordination. What's more, if you haven't exercised in some time, you may be surprised at how physically adept you really are. Also, if you've never been fond of sports, keep in mind that there are countless cardiovascular workouts to choose among—you're bound to find one that suits you. Not all cardiovascular exercises are sports-related. Spinning, step class, and bicycle riding are good cardiovascular workouts that you can do without a group or teammate.

- **Think of exercise as a responsibility.** When you pledge to work out, you're making a promise to yourself that is no less important than a promise you make to a best friend. Write your exercise "appointments" in your calendar, just as you would any commitment, then stick to them. You wouldn't stand up a friend for lunch; don't stand up yourself at your work-out time, either.

- **Seek support.** Physical activity will inevitably take time away from your family, friends, and maybe even co-workers, triggering feelings of guilt that may discourage you from working out. If you let people close to you know how important your work-out time is and how much you need their support to keep you motivated, they're sure to be understanding. Better yet, recruit people to exercise with you. They will make your workouts more enjoyable, plus you'll be more prone to honor your commitment to exercise if a partner is relying on you.

- **Exercise for exercise's sake.** Certainly, physical activity is a means to the end of getting a stronger, slimmer and healthier body. Yet while exercising, forget about your goals and allow yourself to experience the workout. Let your mind wander, daydream, relax, or problem-solve.

Exercise is a wonderful time-out from the real world, but if you're too busy worrying about the physical benefits you're reaping, you won't get the psychological ones. Allow yourself to live in the moment and you'll likely learn to see your workouts not as penance, but as something you actually look forward to.

seven

The Fit Factor Plan

THERE ARE MORE THAN 600 MUSCLES IN THE BODY—and a strength-training exercise for just about every one. But a well-rounded strength-training plan needn't include an overwhelming number of exercises or any complicated, esoteric moves. You can increase your muscle mass and muscle tone, lose weight and improve your health with a relatively simple program.

Enter the **Fit Factor Plan**. If you're like most people these days—short on time, long on life's pressures—the idea of tackling a formalized plan might seem daunting. The beauty of the **Fit Factor Plan** is that it's streamlined. It does require that you set aside time for physical activity, but it's designed to help you get the job done without an overwhelming time commitment.

The **Fit Factor Plan** is made up of three parts:

- **Training for Strength.** Most of these strengthening exercises are done with hand weights, though some depend on your own body weight to challenge the muscles. Since minimum equipment is required, you can do them at home. Given the numerous health and weight loss benefits of building strength, we suggest you embark on this aspect of the program first. Give yourself time to get used to working with weights now and you'll be hooked for the long run.

- **Cardiovascular Conditioning.** The beauty of aerobic workouts is that there are so many of them to choose from. To achieve maximum fitness (and avoid boredom), you might want to work more than one into your routine.

- **The Flexibility Factor.** Stretching is the component of fitness that exercisers, even diligent ones, often forget about. But these six exercises don't require a lot of extra effort. They easily tack on to the beginning and end of your cardiovascular and strength training workouts.

While you've probably done some aerobic exercise (even if it's just walking) and stretches before, strength training with weights may be new territory. For many women, strengthening has long been overlooked as an important fitness component. Strength training not only has its own rewards, it can also compliment your cardiovascular exercise by strengthening the muscles you need to push your legs up a hill or propel your arms through a pool. Almost all athletes now strength train to prepare for their sport, and although you don't need to be a hard body to do so, you'll benefit from taking a page from their playbooks.

Before starting the plan, choose one of the components to focus on at a time instead of all three at once. Begin with the strength training routine. Consider getting involved in an aspect of fitness that traditionally is overlooked, yet is crucially important in terms of losing weight.

Of course, all three components of the **Fit Factor Plan** can be started simultaneously, although the scheduling will be up to you (more on scheduling to come). Remember: This is not a 6-week, 10-week, or even a 12-week program; you should think of physical activity as an ongoing part of your entire life. After you've reached your goal weight, you'll still need to exercise to keep the pounds from creeping back. Consider the **Fit Factor Plan** a way to help you get a new lease on life—a lease that you'll continue to renew again and again. Here's what lies ahead.

The ten exercises included here work the major muscle groups in the upper, lower, and middle sections of the body. Most of them will require that you use free weights (as opposed to weight machines), while others rely on your own body weight. All of the moves are fairly easy to learn and, once you get into the program, it should only take about 30 minutes to complete.

After a few weeks of weight training, you will most likely notice that it's easier to lift your children and the groceries, or to walk up the stairs. You will see muscle definition eventually, but remember: Muscle lies underneath fat, so you may not be able to see the curve of the triceps (the muscle in the back of your upper arm) or depression of the quadriceps (the muscle in the front of your thigh) until you begin to lose weight. But even if definition isn't visible in the beginning, rest assured you're building muscle.

GETTING STARTED, KEEPING GOING

As you begin your workout, the goal should be to perform a strength-training session two to three days a week, skipping at least one day in between. You should also perform at least one set of 8 to 12 repetitions (also called reps) per exercise.

Since each person is different, choose the weight appropriate for you (it may vary from exercise to exercise) by experimenting. If you're able to lift the weight eight times before your muscles fatigue (the last repetitions should feel super-difficult), then it's the right one.

As you get stronger, you'll work up to 12 repetitions. When you are able to complete two consecutive sessions at 12 reps, increase the weight in one- to two-pound increments. Never increase the weight by more than $2^1/2$ pounds. Eventually, you may reach a point where you stop increasing the weight you lift and simply work on maintaining the muscle you've already built.

Be sure to rest about a minute to a minute and a half between sets, if you're doing more than one. Take the same resting time between exercises, too. It's also important that you rest between strength-training workouts. Give your body at least one day between sessions so that your muscles have time to repair the tiny tears that sometimes occur during training.

The Must-Haves for Weight Training

You don't have to spend much money to equip yourself properly for strength training, but you will need a few basics:

- **Sets of hand weights.** Hand weights come in varying weights, starting at one pound, and they can be used for many different exercises. You may want to start with one-pound weights, but you will likely progress quickly, so it might be a good idea to purchase several sets of weights within the range of three-, five-, six-, eight- and ten-pounds. Try them out in the store and choose weights that work for you now, as well as in the weeks to come. Before you buy, hold a few different types in your hand to see which feels most comfortable, as well.

- **A sturdy, armless chair.** You'll be performing some of the exercises while seated so make sure you have a stable chair that is not too deep or shallow.

- **An exercise mat.** This is optional, but it's nice to have a mat for abdominal exercises, especially if you'll be doing them on a hard floor.

- **Comfortable, fitted clothes.** Choose apparel that isn't binding but won't bunch up and get in the way while you're working out. It's not absolutely necessary to wear athletic shoes for weight training, but they offer the best support.

WEIGHT ROOM RULES TO LIVE BY

Remember, you can injure yourself when working out with weights. Rushing your workout or simply not paying attention to your form can both leave you sidelined for weeks. In fact, if you're one of the six million Americans who complain of back pain, you need to be especially vigilant about your weight-lifting techniques. In order to avoid muscle strain or injury, it's essential to use the following safe lifting guidelines.

1. Maintain good posture. Make sure that your back is straight and that your head and neck are in line with your spine. When standing, keep your pelvis tucked under slightly and your knees a little bent.

2. Move the weights in a slow, controlled way. Maintain control both when you raise the weights and when you bring them down; lift on a slow count of two and lower them on a slow count of three.

3. Breathe. As a rule, exhale on the exertion (whether you're lifting a weight or your body) and inhale as you lower down. Be conscious of your breathing and never hold your breath or strain—it restricts blood flow and can make you light-headed.

4. Don't get sloppy. If the exercises are making you so tired that your posture begins to sag or you can only take a weight partially through the full range of motion, either reduce the number of repetitions or lower the weight you're lifting. Never sacrifice good form for more repetitions.

5. Always warm up and cool down. Before you begin your strength-training session, do at least five minutes of aerobic exercise and some easy stretching to warm up your muscles and make them more flexible. The warm-up can be anything that revs up your circulation, such as walking, turning on an aerobics video, or hopping on a cardiovascular machine like the stair climber or stationary bike. When you've completed your strength-training routine, don't forget to stretch out the muscles you've just worked.

THE FIT FACTOR EXERCISES

Although you don't have to do all of these exercises in a single session—you can, for instance, do the upper body exercises on one day and the lower body ones the next—try to do them in the suggested order. It's best to work your smaller muscles (in your arms) after you've worked the bigger muscles (like the buttocks and thighs), since smaller muscles tire more easily, and since you'll need them to help you work the bigger muscles.

Unless otherwise noted, do one set of 8 to 12 repetitions of each exercise.

Squats

Target: The buttock (gluteus), front of the thigh (quadriceps), and back of the thigh (hamstrings) muscles.

The start: Grasp a hand weight in each hand so that your palms face your thighs. Stand in front of a chair with your feet hip-width apart and toes pointing forward.

The move: Keeping your back straight, head up, and eyes forward, slowly bend your knees as if you were going to sit down. Make sure your knees don't extend past your ankles and only lower down as far as you can go (no further than a half squat) without feeling pain. (Ultimate goal: To squat down to the point where your thighs are parallel to the floor.)

The finish: Slowly straighten your knees and rise back up to the starting position.

Step-Ups

Target: The buttock (gluteus), front of the thigh (quadriceps), and back of the thigh (hamstrings) muscles.

The start: Grasp a hand weight in each hand so that your palms face your thighs. Stand in front of a step with your feet hip-width apart and toes pointing forward.

The move: Keeping your back straight, head up, and eyes forward, place your left foot on the step, then your right.

The finish: Step back off with your left, then right foot to starting position.

Calf Raises

Target: The lower leg (gastrocnemius and soleus) muscles.

The start: Grasp a hand weight in each hand so that your palms are facing your thighs. Stand on a step with your feet hip-width apart, your toes pointing forward, and your heels hanging over the edge.

The move: Keeping your back and knees straight, head up, and eyes forward, slowly rise up on your toes.

The finish: Slowly lower your heels as far as comfortably possible. Rise back up again from this position.

Modified Push-Ups

Target: The front of the upper arm (biceps), shoulder (deltoid), and chest (pectoralis major) muscles.

The start: Get down on your hands and knees. Cross your ankles and walk your hands forward so that your body is at a 45 degree angle to the floor and your arms are supporting your weight.

The move: Bend your elbows and lower your body down as far as you can go and still be able to raise back up again. (Ultimate goal: lowering to about one inch from the floor).

The finish: Slowly straighten your arms to raise back up. Do as many as you can. Work up to one set of 20.

Variation: When you get stronger, try to do push-ups with your legs straight and your toes (rather than your knees) resting on the floor. You may also want to try moving your arms wider apart to work other muscles in the shoulders and chest.

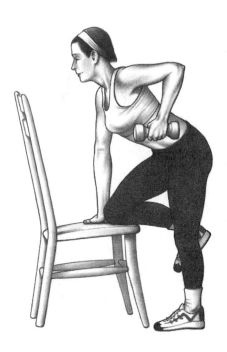

One-Arm Rows

Target: The upper back (latissimus dorsi) and front of the upper arm (biceps) muscles.

The start: Stand with your body bent forward at the waist, and your right knee and right hand resting on a chair or bench. Your right hand should be directly under your shoulder and your right knee under your hip, your back angled over the floor and your shoulders square. Hold a hand weight in your left hand and let your arm hang down.

The move: Contract your abdominal muscles and bend your left elbow, lifting the hand weight until the elbow is higher than your back and the weight is near your underarm. Keep your elbow close to your side throughout the move and use your shoulder and upper back muscles to lift the weight.

The finish: Slowly lower the hand weight back to starting position. Complete one set; switch sides.

Shoulder Presses

Target: The shoulder (deltoid) and back of the upper arm (triceps) muscles.

The start: Stand or sit on a chair or bench. Holding a hand weight in each hand, bend your elbows so the weights are at shoulder level with your palms facing forward.

The move: Keeping your back straight, straighten your arms and slowly raise the hand weights over your head, bringing them together at the top

The finish: Slowly lower back down to the starting position.

Triceps Extensions

Target: The back of the upper arm (triceps) muscles.

The start: Sit on a chair or bench. Hold a hand weight in your right hand, then raise your right arm and bend it at the elbow so that the weight is behind your back. Stabilize your right arm by holding the elbow with your left hand.

The move: Keeping your right elbow close to your ear, slowly raise the hand weight above your head until your right arm is straight.

The finish: Slowly lower down to the starting position. Do one set and switch sides.

Biceps Curls

Target: The front of the upper arm (biceps) muscles.

The start: Grasp a hand weight in each hand so that your palms are facing your thighs. Stand with your feet hip-width apart and toes pointing forward.

The move: Raise both hands and, rotating your wrists, bring the hand weights up toward your shoulders.

The finish: Slowly lower the hand weight to starting position, then repeat the move with your left hand. Continue alternating.

Curl-Ups

Target: The abdominal muscles (rectus abdominis).

The start: Lie on your back with your knees bent, feet flat on the floor. Rest your hands lightly on the front of your knees (or loosely behind your head, as you get stronger).

The move: Squeeze your abdominal muscles and slowly raise your shoulders about 30 degrees off the floor. Don't push yourself forward with your hands; use your abdominal muscles to roll you up and forward.

The finish: Slowly roll back down to the starting position (keep chin tucked in). Do ten. Work up to one set of 20.

Side Sit-Ups

Target: The side abdominal muscles (obliques).

The start: Lie on your back with your knees bent, chin tucked to chest, feet flat on the floor. Place your hands loosely behind your head and let your elbows fall out to the sides so your arms are parallel to the floor.

The move: Squeeze your abdominal muscles, twist slightly to the left and slowly raise your right shoulder toward your left knee (it's not necessary to touch but keep your elbows back and to the side of your head, don't crank your elbow around to the front). Don't push yourself toward your knee with your hands; use your abdominal muscles to pull you up and across.

The finish: Slowly roll back down to the starting position (keep your chin into chest), then repeat the move on the other side. Continue alternating. Do ten on each side. Work up to one set of 20 on each side.

OTHER STRENGTH-TRAINING CONSIDERATIONS

If you're considering investing more in building strength—be it via purchasing home equipment or a health club membership—you have several good options.

The weight-machine alternative

Many gyms offer an array of weight-training machines. If you belong to a club and want to try them, be sure to enlist the help of a qualified trainer to learn how to properly use them. Machines are not as versatile as free weights. Although free weights enable you to work countless muscles in a variety of different ways, weight training machines are safer and often easier to use. Some people also find that a machine workout goes faster than a free-weight session.

Circuit training

One way to take the monotony out of weight training—and reap two workouts in one—is to circuit train. Circuit training involves quickly and continuously moving from one weight "station" (or machine) to another, so it gets the heart rate up, allowing you to work your cardiovascular system and burn more calories as you strengthen your muscles.

Here's how it works: You begin a circuit-training routine by doing one weight-training exercise as many times as possible (at least 15 to 20 with good form) for 30 seconds, rest for 15 seconds, then move on to the next station in the circuit. (To perform this high number of repetitions, you use lighter weights than you normally would if you were doing a traditional strength-training workout.) A circuit training routine can involve anywhere from 8 to 15 stations and the circuit is repeated for 30 to 50 minutes of exercise.

Another way to circuit train is to alternate weight-training stations with aerobic stations such as a treadmill, stair climber or stationary bike. After 30 seconds of weight lifting, you might spend two to three minutes on a cardiovascular machine, then continue alternating until you reach a desired time goal.

Although circuit training doesn't build strength as effectively as traditional weight training, it still conditions the muscles. Also, since it's a fast-paced routine, it leaves little time for boredom while providing the all-important calorie-burning aerobic effect. You can try circuit training on your own or check out the circuit training classes offered at many gyms.

The pros of hiring a pro

Having a personal trainer work with you on an individual basis can be costly—anywhere from $25 to $75 per hour, depending on where you live. However, you don't have to work with a trainer on an ongoing basis. In just a few sessions, a trainer can show you proper weight-lifting form and help you adapt the program in this book to your individual needs.

Several organizations certify trainers, including the American College of Sports Medicine (ACSM), American Council on Exercise (ACE), National Strength and Conditioning Association (NSCA), and the Aerobics and Fitness Association of America (AFAA). Some colleges and universities also give certification to exercise professionals. Look for someone who is not only certified, but has had several years' experience in physical education. The best way to find a personal trainer is through word of mouth. Next best is through a health club—many of them have trainers on staff.

eight

Building a Fit Heart

IT'S IMPORTANT TO REMEMBER THAT it takes time to build aerobic fitness and tone muscles. Remember that getting fit is a process; you'll want to exercise at a pace that you'll be able to stick with for the long-term. Just as it's critical to make healthy eating a regular part of your lifestyle—and not just something you do until you drop a few pounds—your commitment to aerobic exercise needs to be life-long, as well.

If that sounds daunting, bear in mind that you don't need to work out like an Olympic athlete to shed pounds and maintain weight loss. Every minute you spend engaged in cardiovascular exercise—whether it's 20 or 60 minutes—burns calories. Of course, the more time you spend working out, the more calories you'll burn, but if you're starting out with just five minutes of, say, easy walking, don't worry. You'll progress with each passing week and slowly double, then triple the amount of time you spend working up a sweat.

GETTING STARTED, KEEPING GOING

But not everyone *likes* to work up a sweat. Luckily, the beauty of aerobic exercise is that it doesn't have to be strenuous, and the choices are innumerable. Here's what you need to know to get started.

As you embark on your cardiovascular workout, your goal should be 20 to 60 minutes of continuous exercise (with a minimum calorie-burn of 250 to 300 calories per session) at an intensity of 65 to 80 percent of your maximum heart rate, three to five days a week.

What points should I keep in mind?

Naturally, the more time you put into your workouts, the more calories you'll burn. The same is true of intensity—the harder you work out, the bigger the reward. However, increasing the duration or intensity of your sessions too quickly can be self-defeating. It takes time for the body to adapt to the demands you're making on it. Prematurely asking it to perform above a level it's conditioned to handle, can cause you to run out of gas fast. You'll also risk injuring yourself since, as you fatigue, you'll lose good form, which may lead you to make a false, and ultimately, painful move. Even if you're walking, fatigue can make it easier to sprain an ankle or injure a knee.

Whether you're a beginner or someone who has been exercising regularly, you should progress to the next level at an increase of no more than 10 percent per week. You will notice, however, that improvements are not linear; they will likely come readily at the start, then curve off.

There are two ways to make your workouts more physically challenging. One is by increasing the time; the other is by increasing the intensity. For instance, if you usually log two miles on a treadmill (at a ten minute/mile pace) and want to bump up your *intensity* by 10 percent, you could increase your distance to 2.2 miles. But here's the catch: you should cover the new distance in the same 20-minute time period. On the other hand, if you wanted to increase the *duration* of your workout, you could simply stay on the treadmill for an extra two minutes. Even though these increments may seem small, your body will need to adapt to the challenge and the extra calories you burn will begin to add up.

Ultimately, you may want to increase both the duration and the intensity of your workouts, but it may be easier if you begin by adjusting the time. Within six weeks to two months you should be doing at least 20 minutes of aerobic activity, three to five times a week. With that in mind, here's a ten-week schedule you might want to use as a guide. Choose the timetable that works best for your level of expertise. If you had trouble completing the "Test your aerobic ability" challenge on page 61, follow the beginner's schedule.

OUTFITTING YOURSELF

Equipment requirements for aerobic exercise depend on the activity (or activities) you decide to pursue, but here are some general tips.

- **Loose or snug work-out wear?** It really doesn't matter what you wear as long as it feels comfortable and doesn't hamper your movements. Some women prefer to work out in tighter clothes (fitted tank or sports tops, bike shorts, and leggings knit with Lycra), while others prefer baggier clothes (sweat pants, shorts, and T-shirts). Choose fabrics that make you feel good, too. Some synthetic fabrics are made to "wick" sweat off the skin so they stay drier and therefore may chafe less. However, some people like the feel of natural cotton next to the skin.

    One of the most important articles of clothing you'll need for total comfort while working out is a sports bra. There are many types to choose among—bras with and without cups, with Y-backs and with more traditional over-the-shoulder straps. The type of bra you select is a matter of personal preference. You may want to choose one made from a synthetic fabric that wicks perspiration (a sweat-soaked bra can be particularly uncomfortable). In addition, when trying a bra on, move around in the dressing room to get an idea of its supportiveness. A study done by researchers at the University of Wisconsin, La Crosse, on behalf of the American Council on Exercise (ACE), found that some sports bras designed for large-breasted women offer no more support than regular bras, so make sure your bra offers the support you need.

- **Shoes matter.** The concept that you need a different shoe for every activity may seem like a marketing ploy, but there is some reason behind it. A shoe that is constructed with particular moves in mind will likely ease the impact on your feet as well as the rest of your body. Walking shoes, for instance, are more flexible and have more heel support than running shoes; tennis shoes have more give on the sides to accommodate lateral movements. Many companies now make cross-training shoes that are suitable for several activities, but if you plan on doing one type of workout extensively, you may want to purchase a shoe made especially for that sport.

Whenever possible, buy shoes from a store or manufacturer that specializes in athletic footwear, and shop at the end of the day when your feet are the largest. Discuss your needs with the salesperson. If there is any discomfort when you try on the shoes, be wary—it's not likely that the shoes will change much once you start exercising in them.

- **Two worthy accessories.** You also might want to consider two optional, yet helpful items: a heart rate monitor and a waist-pack water-bottle-holder.

  Heart rate monitors allow you to check on whether you're exercising in your target heart rate (THR) without stopping to take your pulse. The best ones have a chest strap that measures your heart rate, then transmits it to a watch-like device on your wrist. Better models run about $100. Heart rate monitors are really great because they allow you to take a direct look at your engine—your heart. It really helps you to monitor what heart rate range you're working in and is far more effective and accurate than taking your pulse.

  A heart rate monitor may seem like an unnecessary tool, but it might be one of the best ones a beginning exerciser can buy. It allows you to work out more efficiently because you know and maintain your THR simply and effectively. You may notice that you'll lose more weight working out with a heart rate monitor even though your workout time doesn't increase because you are maximizing your exercise time and making it more effective. If you want to take aerobic exercising seriously, it is a great tool to have.

It's essential to stay hydrated while you're engaged in cardiovascular exercise (more on hydrating in chapter 11), so it's a good idea to carry a bottle of calorie-free, thirst-quenching water. Waist packs make drinking up a lot more convenient: They free up your hands and you'll never be caught high and dry while working out.

- **Think twice before buying home exercise gadgets.** You don't really need tons of expensive equipment to outfit a

---

What's in a Walking Shoe?

Since most of us walk in every type of shoe we have, from high heels to bedroom slippers, it may seem like any shoe will do. But when you get out there and start walking briskly for extended periods of time, you'll need a shoe with plenty of support and durability. Here's what to look for:

- **The right amount of cushioning.** In general, people with low-arched feet require shoes with less cushioning, but more support and heel control. High-arched feet need more shock absorption and thus greater cushioning than do people with lower-arched feet. You don't, however, want to get a shoe that has too much cushioning, since thicker soles make a shoe less flexible. As you walk, your foot flexes at about a 45 degree angle, rolls through the step, then flexes again as you bring it forward. With all this flexing going on, you need a shoe that "gives," which is why most shoes made specifically for walking have fairly thin and flexible soles. The soles of running shoes, on the other hand, are a lot thicker and much less flexible since runners' feet don't flex as much and they need the extra cushioning.

- **A lot of rubber on the outside.** The more rubber that's affixed to the outsole of the shoe, the more durable a shoe is likely to be.

- **Supportive uppers.** A wobbly foot can cause ankle or knee problems, so you want a shoe that keeps your foot stable. A stiff plastic upper in the heel area will also help keep your foot steady as you go.

home gym. A jump rope, a few aerobic exercise tapes, and a bench for stepping will suffice, as will a few hand weights for your strength-training routine.

If you're dazzled by the fitness gadget ads you see on television, consider this: Researchers in the Department of Kinesiology at California State University, Northridge discovered fitness gadgets may not do the job any better than exercise done without equipment. They had nine men and ten women test out four of the best-selling abdominal trainers. Each subject performed four different muscle movements, depending on the particular instructions accompanying the device. Using a technique called electromyography to measure the electrical activity of the participants' muscle groups, the researchers concluded that the devices worked the muscles no better than plain old abdominal exercises. When it comes to home treadmills, stair climbers, rowing machines, stationary bikes, cross-country ski machines, and the like, think hard before you buy. As many know, home machines often become expensive clothes racks.

If you do decide to buy one, keep in mind that there's a strong correlation between price and quality in home exercise equipment. Still, some stores set their prices higher than others, so shop around. Always try out the machine before buying and be sure that it comes with a warranty and service plan.

CARDIOVASCULAR CONDITIONING GOALS

What about pace?

As noted, your ultimate goal should be to work out at an intensity of 65 to 80 percent of your maximum heart rate (MHR). Or, on the scale of rate of perceived exertion (RPE) somewhere around 13 or 14, a rating that puts the exercise at "somewhat hard." If, however, you're a beginner who has a poor level of fitness, exercise at a lower intensity—40 to 50 percent of you MHR (RPE rating of "fairly light")—at a pace that will leave you just barely breaking a sweat. As you get more

WEEKS	TIME IN MINUTES (BEGINNER)	TIME IN MINUTES (INTERMEDIATE)	TIME IN MINUTES (ADVANCED)
1	10	20	30
2	11	22	33
3	12	24	36
4	13	26	40
5	14	29	44
6	15	32	48
7	16	35	53
8	18	39	58
9	20	43	60
10	22	47	60

fit, you'll need to increase the intensity. In the beginning, 40 to 50 percent of your MHR will challenge your cardiovascular system, helping your body to both burn calories and increase its aerobic fitness.

Whatever your work-out pace, once it becomes less difficult and seems light, it's time to raise the intensity of your sessions. But, as with increasing duration, follow the ten-percent rule when increasing intensity. For instance, if you're exercising at a heart rate of 50 percent MHR and are ready to work a little harder, only nudge the pace up to 55 percent of your MHR.

How can I tell if I've increased the pace more than I should?

If you can't carry on a normal conversation while you're exercising, you're working too hard. Your workout shouldn't leave you gasping for breath. It shouldn't speed up to the point where you have trouble speaking or rate the exercise as feeling more than "somewhat hard."

How long before I see results?

If you're exercising at least three times weekly, you should begin to see some weight loss and a change in your aerobic ability in about four

Does Slow and Steady Win the Fat-Burning Race?

One of the common misconceptions about exercise is that you will lose more body fat if you exercise at a slow pace than if you exercise at a fast pace. Here's the truth: About 30 to 80 percent of the fuel for exercise is derived from stored body fat; the rest is largely from carbohydrates. If your exercise is slow-paced, you *will* burn closer to the 80 percent mark than if you were working out at a higher intensity. However, if your exercise is fast-paced you'll end up burning more calories overall—including fat calories. Thus, ultimately, you'll net a higher fat burn-off with higher-intensity exercise. But this doesn't mean you should work out frantically: Exercise too strenuously and you won't be able to keep it up long enough to expend a substantial amount of energy—or have any fun. Worse, you may injure yourself if you're working beyond your body's capabilities and then you won't be able to exercise at all.

weeks. You'll likely begin to feel more energetic immediately, but it will take a few weeks before you notice that everyday activities, like climbing the stairs, get easier and that your clothes feel a little looser.

EIGHT EXCELLENT AEROBIC OPTIONS

The beauty of cardiovascular exercise is that there are so many options—and all of them burn calories, challenge your cardiovascular system, and build aerobic fitness, to some degree. There really is no "best" aerobic activity, but there is a best activity (or activities) for you: It is the one (ones) you like. If you enjoy your workouts, you'll be much more apt to become a regular exerciser.

If you like more than one activity, cross training—or regularly varying your cardiovascular routine—has several advantages. Most importantly, circuit training reduces the risk of injuries since you won't be as likely to overwork your muscles if you're not continually repeating the same motion over and over. Cross training also enables you to firm, tone, and aerobically train various areas of the body and, because it breaks up what might otherwise be a monotonous routine, keeps exercise interesting.

The ideal way to cross train is to pair workouts that primarily work the upper body with ones that challenge the lower body: alternating walking and swimming, for instance; or using the stair climber at the gym on one day, the rowing machine the next. If you're up for it, your cross-training program could include running, cycling, kickboxing, and in-line skating. You can also cross train within one workout by, say, doing ten minutes on the treadmill, ten minutes on the stationary bike, and ten minutes on the stair climber.

To help you decide which activities suit you best, here are descriptions of five old standbys, plus three newer workouts that are gaining in popularity.

1. Walking

One of the many things that walking has going for it—besides the fact that it burns calories and tones leg muscles—is that it's a low-impact exercise. Even when you're walking at a brisk pace, the wear-and-tear on your joints is minimal, but it's still a weight-bearing exercise, so it's good for the bones. Walking is also the most accessible of all workouts. You can do it anywhere, wear almost anything (although walking shoes are recommended), and there's virtually no learning curve. Still, there is some technique involved in walking at a speedy pace. You don't need to adopt the somewhat awkward motions of race-walkers, but here are a few things to bear in mind:

* **Stand tall, body relaxed.** Think of lengthening your body from your toes up to the top of your head, but without straining. Stand tall, but not stiffly.

* **Head up.** The way you hold your head can affect your entire body. If you hold it down or tuck your chin under, your shoulders are likely to round, with improper alignment and bad posture following in their wake. As you walk, keep your eyes focused straight ahead, your chin lifted and your neck tall—the rest of your body will fall in line.

* **Shoulders back and down, chest up.** Relax your shoulders down away from your ears, then pull them slightly back, opening up your chest. As your chest opens, allow it to lift, as if there were a string attached to your breastbone pulling up.

Walking into High Gear

Walking at any speed can help you lose weight, but if you want to maximize your energy expenditure, it pays to work on increasing your walking speed. Fast walking not only burns more calories than slow walking, it keeps your metabolism elevated for a longer period of time post-exercise.

If you can walk continuously for at least 40 minutes, you're ready to begin adding some speed training to your routine. One way to build speed is to insert short, fast segments into your walking workouts. Known as interval training (in between the fast segments you walk at a more moderate pace), these types of workouts challenge your heart and lungs enough to build fitness, but also let your body recover before you get overtired. As your body adapts to the faster intervals, you'll be able to walk at a rapid pace for longer periods of time.

The following workouts will not only help you burn more calories, they'll help keep your walking sessions interesting. Since they can be fairly taxing, only do them three days a week, alternating them with your usual walks. Note: Interval training isn't only used by walkers. You can incorporate these fast-slow intervals into any steady-state type of exercise, be it swimming, cycling, running, or working out on a cardiovascular machine.

SPONTANEOUS SPEED PLAY

This workout lets you add "speed bursts" whenever the spirit moves you.

1. Warm up by walking at your normal pace for ten minutes.

2. Speed up so that on an exertion scale of one to ten, with ten as your top walking speed, you are at about a seven.

3. When you start to tire, slow down to a level of about four.

4. Repeat as many times as comfortably possible during your regular walking distance.

5. Cool down and stretch.

❋ **Abdominal muscles pulled in.** The abdominal muscles are the body's core, helping to keep everything else in line. By contracting and pressing them back towards your spine, you are helping to support your lower back and keep your entire body lifted.

THE LADDER

Start with as many speed bursts as feels comfortable, and gradually work up to eight to ten. As the workout becomes easier, increase the length of the speed burst by five seconds each week.

1. Warm up by walking at your normal pace for ten minutes.

2. Walk as fast as you can for 30 seconds.

3. Slow to your normal pace for two minutes.

4. Repeat as many times as possible during your regular walking distance.

5. Cool down and stretch.

THE PYRAMID

In this workout, speeding up should bring your pace to a seven on an exertion scale of one to ten. Slowing down means returning to your normal walking pace, about a five on the scale.

1. Warm up by walking at your normal pace for ten minutes.

2. Speed up for one minute, slow down for one minute.

3. Speed up for two minutes, slow down for two minutes.

4. Speed up for three minutes, slow down for three minutes.

5. Speed up for three minutes, slow down for three minutes.

6. Speed up for two minutes, slow down for two minutes.

7. Speed up for one minute, slow down for one minute.

8. Cool down and stretch.

❈ **Natural stride.** To determine a proper, comfortable pace, lean forward from your hips and ankles (not your waist) and fall forward, breaking the fall by stepping forward. The distance between your feet is the length of your natural stride.

❋ **Arm swing.** Surprisingly, your arms have as much to do with how fast you go as your feet. The feet *follow* the arms. To correctly position your arms, bend them at a 90 degree angle at the elbows, then pump them forward and back as you move. Keep your hands closed (but not clenched) and arms close to your torso. As you pump your arms, don't allow your hands to swing back beyond your hips or forward and up past your sternum.

At some point, if you walk fast enough, you may want to switch to running. Running isn't as easy on the body as walking, but it burns more calories per hour. If running isn't for you, consider increasing the effectiveness of your walking workouts with some speed-building variations (see box on pages 98 to 99).

2. Cycling

Cycling is another way to get your heart and lungs working and firm up your legs and butt without putting much stress and strain on your joints. You don't need a sophisticated bike to enjoy the benefits of cycling, although if you plan on eventually riding hills (a great way to increase the challenge of your workout), you may want to get a bike with several gears. Also make certain that your bike *fits* you (the seat and handlebars are adjusted to your height and length) and is adjusted to accommodate your particular body. A bike that's too big or too small or off in some way can make cycling uncomfortable and leave you with a sore back and knees.

One thing to think about if you plan to cycle is that, to reap maximum calorie-burning and cardiovascular benefits, you'll want to be able to ride at a fairly continuous pace. When you map out a route, try to choose one that won't require you to frequently stop and start again. Naturally, also try to choose a route that's safe, and *always* wear a helmet, no matter where you'll be riding.

As you ride, keep your upper body relaxed and maintain a light grip on the handlebars. Also remember to keep the tension on the pedals fairly light so that your legs go around fast. Cycling with a lot of tension can strain knees and make you tire so quickly that you could end up coasting most of the workout or prematurely heading for home.

3. Aerobics

If you have a hard time initially following step or any other type of aerobics, concentrate on mastering the foot movements first, then add in the arm moves. Be aware that raising your arms above shoulder level makes your heart work harder. If the moves are making you feel too breathless, keep your arms low or omit the arm moves all together.

Dance: Anyone who likes to move to music, generally appreciates aerobic dance, whether it be at an exercise studio with a live teacher or at home following a video instructor on television. Most aerobic dance routines combine both arm and leg movements so they provide a great way to get an all-over workout.

Step: The majority of classes taught today are low-impact aerobics—that is, they don't require any jumping and, with each move, you have at least one foot on the ground. These days, many of the most popular aerobic classes (and videotapes) are step aerobics: According to the American Council on Exercise, over ten million people have tried "step." This variation on the theme involves stepping up and down on a platform as well as performing dance moves on and around the step.

4. Swimming

The best exercise around for people with joint problems, swimming has the distinction of being the lowest-impact activity. With water to buoy your movements, joint stress stays minimal. But just because swimming is easy on the joints doesn't mean it's easy on fat. As long as you do it at a pace that gets your heart rate elevated, swimming burns a substantial number of calories. Swimming also is one of the few popular forms of exercise that works both the upper and lower body (though it works the upper body the most).

Some exercisers balk at swimming laps, bored by moving back and forth with no change of scenery, but there are many ways to spice up a swim workout. You can, for instance, vary your strokes or spend some of your lap time using pool tools. One of the most popular is the kickboard, a foam board that floats your upper body so that you can propel yourself across the pool with your legs. Kicking allows you

Profile in Fitness

NAME: DINA A.

OCCUPATION: HOUSEWIFE

HOME STATE: NEW YORK

AGE: 39 YEARS OLD

BEFORE WEIGHT: 279 LBS

AFTER WEIGHT: 155 LBS

HEIGHT: 5'8"

HOW SHE STAYS STRONG AND FIT:

WALKING, 8 MILES PER DAY

SPINNING AND STRETCHING CLASSES, STRENGTH TRAINING

✸

*"...This kind of regimen does great things for my body...
I'm losing inches without losing weight. Everything's toning up.
Plus, I have a lot of endurance now in anything I do."*

Having three children under four years of age, I was basically homebound, and my eating habits suffered for it. I ate whatever they didn't—and more on top of that. The weight started piling on and I was miserable. I had so much weight to lose, it felt impossible. I had always been active; I had even been a fitness instructor fifteen years earlier. To be so heavy simply wasn't me.

I thought, "Let me try Weight Watchers. At least it'll get me out of the house for an hour." Following the Program's recommendations, I started walking, a little at first—not even a mile. I eventually worked up to eight miles, which I still do every day for two hours. At the gym, I take spin and stretch classes, and work with the weight machines. A routine like that goes great together—the stretching, the cardiovascular exercises, and the walking. Every aspect of the workout enhances another, ensuring the greatest benefits.

There's no doubt, this kind of regimen does great things for my body. When I lost 100 pounds, yes, I looked slimmer, but I also looked flabbier at first. By exercising, I'm losing inches without losing weight. Everything's toning up. Plus, I have a lot of endurance now in anything I do.

It also does great things for my head—opening up my mind and clearing my thinking for the rest of the day. I get a natural rush from it. The bottom line is, I like how I feel after exercising: I feel healthy and alive.

to concentrate on toning your legs while working your cardiovascular system at the same time. Fins can also add variety to your routine. Swimming with fins is a little bit like walking with ankle weights: The fins create resistance, making your muscles work harder—and thus get stronger—as you kick. At the same time, fins increase your speed, which can make swimming a lot of fun.

There are also tools that let you concentrate on your upper body. Paddles, rectangle or oval pieces of plastic that slip onto your hands, increase the resistance to your arm, shoulder, back, and chest muscles. They are sometimes used together with pull buoys, floats that, placed between your legs, keep you from kicking so you work only your upper body.

If you like the water, but aren't attracted to swimming, you might consider aqua aerobics. These classes, taught at many pools and Y's around the country, have the dance-feel of aerobics, but because the moves take place in the water, there is less impact on your joints.

5. *Cardiovascular machines*

If you belong to a gym (or have invested in home equipment), you can get an excellent machine-assisted workout. Some people actually prefer indoor exercise to outdoor, since it can be done in any weather and without the interference of cars, stop signs, smog, and other interruptions or hazards. Many people also like the fact that most machines provide information, such as how fast and far you're traveling, and how many calories you're burning.

Each exercise machine has something to recommend it. Here's what to consider before climbing on. Check with a personal trainer to learn how to use equipment properly.

- **Treadmill.** Walking or running on a treadmill burns about the same number of calories as walking or running on pavement, but because the machines have some shock-absorption, treadmill walking and running have less impact on the joints. Most treadmills also have an incline feature that allows you to simulate going up hills. The steeper you raise the incline, the more demand it will make on your cardiovascular system as well as the muscles in the backs of your thighs, butt, and hips.

- **Stair climber.** If you've ever climbed a super-long flight of stairs, you know what it's like to work out on a stair climber. Like real stair climbing, the machine targets the muscles in the butt and thighs while giving your body an aerobic challenge.

  Depending on how hard you want to exercise, a stair climber's pedals can be adjusted to provide varying degrees of resistance. Some machines have programs that will automatically change the resistance to give you an interval workout (where you speed up your pace for short periods of time). To have the best possible session on a stair climber, stand upright (rather than leaning forward) and don't grip the handrails (hold them lightly). By gripping the handrails, you "hang" your weight onto the machine, lowering the amount of weight you carry with each step—and consequently lowering the amount of calories you burn, too.

- **Stationary bicycle.** Before the modern day exercise machines with all their bells and whistles, there was the stalwart stationary bike. Although today's bikes are more technologically advanced, they still produce a good calorie-burning, thigh-toning workout. Like a road or mountain bike, a stationary bike should be adjusted to fit your body to avoid causing you any knee and back aches and pains. If you're thinking about getting a stationary bike for home, consider that you can buy an inexpensive bike stand that allows you to ride your outdoor bicycle as an indoor vehicle.

- **Rowing machine.** Although rowing may seem like a purely upper-body endeavor, you do, in fact, use both your upper and lower body, so it's a great total-body exercise. Generally, you hold on to a handle attached to a cable and fly wheel with both hands, then alternate pulling the handle to glide you forward and using your legs to drive you back. Although the motion is certainly repetitive, many rowing machine aficionados are able to keep it interesting by working on both their stroke rate (the amount of strokes they're able to pull per minute) and their power (how hard they're able to pull the handle).

- **Cross-country ski machine.** Unlike outdoor cross-country skiing, the indoor version is a year-round sport. Most machines involve gliding your feet (clipped into two sliding "skis") back and forth while moving your arms in sync. Your legs get the brunt of the exercise, but cross country ski machines also work the arms—though you may want to wait until you get the hang of the leg movements before adding in the arms.

- **Elliptical trainer.** The newest machine on the block, the elliptical trainer has quickly become a favorite at gyms around the country. This low-impact machine generally involves walking in an oval pattern, which works more muscles in the body than just straightforward walking. Some models also have moveable poles that help work the arms and incline adjustments.

6. Kickboxing

Once solely the domain of Rocky-esque athletes, boxing—and, in particular, kickboxing—has become a popular recreational pursuit for both women and men. Many gyms now offer "cardio kickboxing" classes, and there are an increasing number of punch-and-kick exercise videos (like Tae Bo) on the market. The workout generally consists of a combination of upper-body moves like jabs and uppercut punches and lower-body moves such as roundhouse and front and back kicks. Conditioning moves like jumping jacks and rope jumping are also integrated into the workout.

Kickboxing is an excellent calorie burner and has been shown to increase strength and flexibility, improve coordination, and sharpen reflexes. Perhaps best of all, it's fun: Many women find it a refreshing break from traditional exercise.

7. Spinning

Riding a stationary bike is great exercise, but to some people it's exceedingly boring. Enter spinning (sometimes called indoor cycling), a class where instructors lead exercisers through a vigorous cycling workout to the sound of motivational, energetic music. Spinning bikes have a resistance knob that allows you to adjust the pedals incrementally without the jerkiness of a fixed gear drive. That, and the fact that some classes require cycling shoes, make spinning seem more like an actual outdoor ride than riding a traditional stationary bike.

During the class, you may stand up and pedal part of the time while the instructor has spinners gradually increase the resistance to simulate climbing hills. Other times, you'll be asked to remove some resistance and pump your legs as fast as possible, as if riding downhill. All this variation keeps the ride interesting and, not incidentally, strengthens the thighs and butt muscles. Although such a vigorous class may seem daunting at first, you are always in control of the resistance and how fast you feel comfortable pedaling. However, spinning isn't recommended for beginning exercisers. Wait until you've got a few months of cardiovascular workouts under your belt before giving it a try.

8. In-line skating

If you haven't put on a pair of skates since you were a kid, you might want to check out in-line skating. Working out on in-line skates (or even an old-fashioned pair with the wheels in traditional alignment) is great cardiovascular exercise and strengthens the muscles in the ankles, knees, and hips.

Before buying skates, try renting them—along with protective gear—a few times to see if you like the activity. Find a flat unobstructed spot for your first go around. Different skates have different braking systems, but many have a stop pad on the heel of the right skate. Consider taking a skating class to learn the in-line basics—the sooner you learn proper technique and how to master stopping, the sooner you'll be able to get a steady, aerobic workout going.

THE CALORIE-BURNING PAYOFF

When you read the following calorie-burning chart, keep in mind that some of the calculations—the ones for sports like basketball and soccer, for instance—are based on constant participation. In reality, you may be starting and stopping as you play these sports, so you won't burn quite as many calories. Even so, this should give you some idea of your overall energy expenditure.

ACTIVITY	CALORIES BURNED PER HOUR (BASED ON 150-LB WOMAN)
Basketball	564
Bowling	396
Canoeing (leisurely)	180
Cycling (9.4 mph)	408
Dancing, aerobic (medium pace)	420
Dancing, ballroom	210
Elliptical trainer (medium pace)	540
Frisbee	408
Golf	348
Jumping rope (70 per minute)	660
Karate	798
Kickboxing	498
Racquetball	726
Rowing machine (medium pace)	486
Running (11 mins per mile)	552
Running (9 mins per mile)	792
Skiing (moderate speed, on snow)	486
Skiing machine (medium pace)	564
Spinning (fast pace)	936
Soccer	558
Softball	282
Stair climbing machine (medium pace)	680
Squash	864
Swimming, crawl (slow)	522
Swimming, crawl (fast)	636
Tennis	444
Volleyball	204
Walking, outdoors (leisurely pace)	324
Walking, treadmill (3 mph)	300
Walking, treadmill (4 mph)	396

*Chart adapted from Exercise Physiology, *Fourth Edition, by William D. McArdle, Frank I. Katch and Victor L. Katch (Williams & Wilkins).*

Sports for Weight Loss

These days, the term "soccer mom" could refer not just to moms cart-ing their kids from game to game, but to moms who play soccer themselves. More and more women are incorporating sports into their lives. You may wonder, however, if playing sports is enough to help you lose weight.

It can be if you play often and hard enough. When played by recreational athletes, however, many sports—tennis, squash, soccer, and basketball, just to name a few—don't keep you moving consis-tently enough to burn as many calories as say, continuous walking or stair climbing. They also don't keep your heart rate up long enough to substantially build cardiovascular endurance.

Yet playing sports, even those like golf (if you walk the course) does burn calories and they are a good adjunct to your regular aer-obic and strength training workouts. In fact, sports and conditioning exercise should go hand in hand: Building up your cardiovascular sys-tem and improving your muscle strength will help improve your sports performance.

WARMING UP AND COOLING DOWN

Warming up and cooling down are essential to a complete workout. When you carve out a chunk of time for cardiovascular exercise, be sure to tack on at least five minutes (more if possible) at both ends of the workout for a warm-up and cool-down—even if that means you'll have less time to engage in the faster-paced segment of your workout.

A warm-up is very slow-paced aerobic exercise, like walking or gentle biking; your warm-up choice should engage the same muscles you will be using during your workout. If you're a walker, for instance, you might stroll for five to ten minutes before moving into a brisker-speed walk. If you're a cyclist, pedal slowly before increasing your effort. The benefits of taking the time to warm up are numer-ous: it raises the temperature of your body and increases blood flow to the muscles, which reduces the risk of injury ("cold" muscles are more prone to strains and tears than "warm" ones); it also makes exer-cise less laborious. Muscles that are warmed up are more accepting to movement (think of how much more elastic rubber becomes when it's heated). Since higher body temperatures facilitate the delivery of oxygen, warm muscles are also better fueled. In addition, a warm-up properly prepares the heart muscle and its blood supply for the more intense exercise that lies ahead.

Although you may be to tempted to head for the shower as soon as your aerobic session is finished, don't skip cooling down, either. A cool-down should be tacked onto the end of your workout in order to help your body recover from exercise. If you don't bother to cool down, you run the risk of having your blood pool in various areas of the body, which can cause you to feel dizzy or faint. A few minutes of light exercise will redirect your blood to its normal pattern and, if you've worked out strenuously enough to accumulate lactic acid (a by-product of hard exercise that causes muscle fatigue), help flush it from your bloodstream. After you've cooled down, complete your workout by stretching. (See the following chapter for the details.)

nine

Becoming Flexible

STRETCHING IS EASY AND SHOULD BE PAINLESS. But many people give flexibility exercises the short shrift, perhaps because stretching doesn't produce the kind of visual results that motivate you to exercise. Stretching, that is, doesn't make your muscles firmer or your thighs slimmer.

At least not directly. Stretching actually does have something to do with weight loss: By helping to keep the muscles and joints limber, it makes participating in both aerobic exercise and strength training easier—and safer. A limber muscle is less likely to tear and put you on the sidelines than one that hasn't been stretched. Also, stretching your muscles after you work out actually makes them stronger, up to 15 percent, than if you didn't stretch at all.

Although some kinds of stretching come naturally—most of us do a little bit every morning as we prepare to get out of bed—there is some technique required for more formal types of exercise. (Much as stretching can help prevent injury, it can also *cause* injury if done incorrectly.)

Coming up are ten stretches that hit every major muscle group in the body. But before you put in some flex time, read about the basics of stretching to make sure you do them properly.

GETTING STARTED, KEEPING GOING

As you begin a flexibility routine, you should aim for completing a set of ten stretches at least two to three times a week, before and after an aerobic or strength training workout.

How does stretching work?

Typically, when you rapidly stretch a muscle more than it can comfortably go, sensitive structures within the muscle cells known as "spindles" spring into action. They fire off a message to the brain, which causes the muscle to contract. This process is called the stretch reflex and it's responsible for that slight discomfort you feel as you first move into a stretch. When you stretch repeatedly and slowly, however, the spindles learn to tolerate the tension and allow you to extend the muscles further.

When is the best time to stretch?

For years, experts debated whether it was better to stretch before or after exercise—or both. The consensus seems to be that it's better to stretch after exercise, not only because cold muscles are more prone to strain, but also because adding stretching to a cool-down routine helps keep the muscles from stiffening up after exercise. However, a mild pre-exercise stretch is also beneficial if you take 5 or 10 minutes to warm up your muscles first (by, say, walking or peddling a bike).

The times you stretch shouldn't be limited to working out, either. Stretching daily will help make your everyday moves easier and loosen up muscles (particularly back muscles) after you've been sitting or standing for long periods of time. If you're going to stretch without exercising first, warm up by doing five to ten minutes of light cardiovascular moves.

What's the best way to stretch?

The stretches in this program are known as "static" stretches because they involve slowly extending yourself to the point where you can feel tension (but not pain) in a particular muscle, then holding the position for an extended period of time. (You may have seen people perform stretches in a "ballistic" fashion—bouncing rather than holding a position. This is not recommended because it puts so much strain on the muscles and joints and rapidly triggers the counter-acting stretch reflex.)

Although you may only be able to hold the move for a few seconds at first, over time you should be able to work up to 40 seconds. Remember to keep breathing as you hold each stretch and think of extending into the stretch even further with each exhale.

TEN FLEXIBILITY ENHANCERS

Unless otherwise noted, hold these stretches for 20 to 40 seconds. Always move gently into position and never stretch to the point of pain.

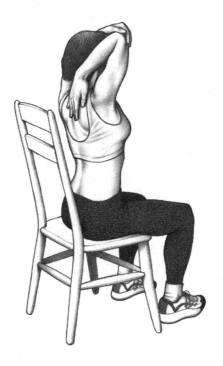

1. Upper arm (triceps) stretch

Raise your right arm, then bend it so that your hand drops behind your back (but your head should not drop forward). Place your left hand on your right elbow and gently pull your right arm toward your head until you feel a good stretch in your upper-arm muscles (triceps). Repeat on the other side.

2. Shoulder stretch

Extend your left arm in front of you at chest level. Grab your left arm at the elbow joint with your right arm and gently pull your arm across your chest until you feel a good stretch in your shoulder. Repeat on the other side.

3. Chest and shoulder stretch

Stand straight and interlace your fingers behind your back. Gently lift your hands up until you feel a stretch in your chest and shoulders.

4. Abdominal stretch

Lie on your stomach with your hands by your shoulders (as if you were going to do a push-up). Keeping your legs on the floor and, grounding your pelvis, gently raise your upper body until you feel a good stretch in your abdomen.

5. Hamstring stretch

Sit on the floor with your left leg extended in front of you, your right leg bent so that the sole of your right foot touches the inside of your left thigh. Slowly bend forward at your hips over your left leg and lightly grasp your shin or, if you can, foot, until you feel a good stretch in the back of your thigh. Repeat on the other side.

6. Groin stretch

Sit on the floor with your knees bent and the soles of your feet together in front of you. Hold onto the tops of your feet and, bending at the hips, gently pull yourself forward until you feel a good stretch in your groin.

7. Lower back and hip stretch

Lie on your back with both arms stretched out straight at shoulder height.
Bend your right knee at a 90 degree angle, place your left hand on your
right thigh and pull it over your left leg toward the floor until you feel a good
stretch in your back and hip. Turn your head to the right. Repeat on the other
side.

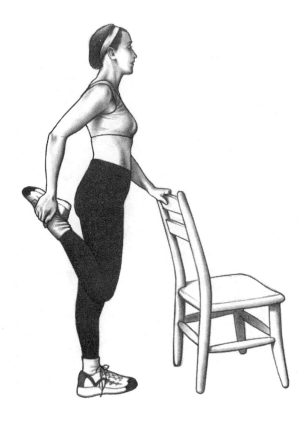

8. Front of thigh (quadriceps) stretch

Stand with your left hand braced on a wall or chair. Bend your right knee, raising the foot up behind you and bring your right hand around to meet it. Keeping your knees close together, grasp your right foot with your right hand and push back gently with your thigh until you feel a stretch in the front. Hold for 20 to 40 seconds. Release your right hand, brace it on the wall or chair and grasp your right foot with your left hand. Again, push back gently with your thigh until you feel a stretch in the front. Hold for 20 to 40 seconds. Repeat on the other side.

9. Calf stretch

Stand several feet away from a wall, then lean forward and place your forearms flat against the wall. Bend your right leg and bring it forward to a 90 degree angle. Lean into the wall until you feel a good stretch in your calf muscle. Repeat on the other side.

10. Back stretch

Kneel on all fours with your toes facing backward. Contract your abdominal muscles and round your back like a cat. Hold ten seconds. Relax your abdominal muscles, push your chest forward and arch your back. Hold ten seconds. Repeat ten times.

GOING OM: YOGA FOR FLEXIBILITY

In the past few years, people interested in fitness have been taking up yoga with a fervor. While this workout of poses has been around for roughly 6,000 years, it fits right in with some of our modern-day goals.

The one it addresses the best is flexibility. Because many of the poses in yoga involve stretching, it helps lengthen the muscles and limber up the joints. Yet, contrary to popular belief, you don't need to be extremely flexible to do yoga: There are many, many variations on the poses, and a good teacher will be able to show you how to master them no matter how flexible you are.

Yoga also offers benefits besides increased flexibility. Since some of the poses require lifting or holding up your own body weight, yoga helps build strength and tone the muscles. And some types, usually billed as ashtanga or power yoga, are practiced at a rapid pace so they help improve cardiovascular fitness, too.

But for all its physical demands, yoga is still a mental discipline. Each move requires mental concentration and much emphasis is placed on mindful breathing as a way to both calm the body (when you start to huff and puff too hard) and muster up the energy you need to perform the poses (when your strength begins to sag). Attention to breathing also keeps your mind centered on what you're doing, allowing you to forget your usual cares and woes. To some devotees, yoga is the best form of stress reduction going.

Many yoga classes have a spiritual component to them, which depending on your outlook, can be a plus or a minus. But whether you could take the chanting or leave it, you're likely to be able to find a class or yoga videotape that suits your style if you take the time to experiment. In the meantime, you might want to try a simple yoga series on your own. The following moves, to be done in a continuous sequence, are part of a traditional yoga practice called the Sun Salutation.

1. Stand tall with your head aligned over your spine, feet together and palms together in prayer position in front of your chest. Activate your legs by pressing your heels into the ground and tightening your thighs. Roll your shoulders back so your chest comes forward.

2. Inhale, sweep your arms out to the side, then bring them up above your head till your palms meet in prayer position. In one continuous motion, exhale, bring your arms back out to the side, bend at the hips and, keeping your back flat, lower your upper body toward the floor.

3. At the point where your upper body and legs form a right angle, allow your back to round, bend your knees slightly, drop your head over your legs and let your arms hang toward the floor (your hands don't have to touch the floor). Inhale and with your arms still reaching toward the floor, arch your back, press your chest forward and lift your head so that your upper body is parallel to the floor. Exhale and round your back again, dropping your torso over your legs and letting your arms hang toward the floor. Inhale, bend your knees until you can place your palms flat on the floor.

4. Step back with your left foot, keeping your right leg bent in a 90 degree angle (knees should be directly over the ankle). Hold for a breath.

5. Then step your right foot back so that you are raised up on your hands and toes in a "plank" position (it looks like the up part of a push-up). From plank, bend your elbows, keeping them close to your sides, and lower your body an inch from the floor (as you would a push-up).

6. Exhale and move into a position called "upward-facing dog": push up with your arms (palms are still flat on the floor), slide your chest forward and roll your toes under so the tops of your feet are on the floor. Stretch back with your heels and forward with your chest so that your upper back bends. Keep your shoulders pulling down and your thighs taut.

7.   Inhale, and pressing your palms on the floor, lift your hips to come into an upside down V—a position called "downward-facing dog." Your palms should still be flat on the floor and your heels pushing downward (the goal is to get the soles of your feet flat on the floor, but don't worry if you can't). Think of your hands and feet as anchors as your butt lifts upwards. Hold for five breaths. On an exhale, walk your feet to your hands and stand up, your torso still folded over your legs. Inhale and arch up as you did in #3, then exhale and fold over your legs again. Inhale, raise your arms out to your side and come up with a flat back, bringing your arms above your head. Exhale, lower your arms and bring them back into prayer position at your chest.

Repeat this sequence five times.

A BETTER BACK

If you are one of the estimated 6,000,000 people who visit their physician each year because of back pain, you may be surprised (and frustrated) to learn that your doctor can't tell you exactly what's wrong. Studies show that less than 10 percent of people seen for back problems show clear evidence of having something like a herniated disk or fracture causing their pain.

Yet, while they can't always pinpoint the exact source of discomfort, experts generally attribute the majority of backaches to muscle strain—and the muscle strains, in turn, to one or a combination of many different actions and conditions. Those most likely to set you up for back pain:

- **Improper lifting.** The most dangerous way to lift is to bend over at the waist, stiff-legged, and hoist, which can overstress the upper and lower back muscles. A better way: Spread your feet shoulder-width to give yourself a good base of support, then bend your knees, pick up the object with your head erect, and raise yourself up with your leg muscles.

- **Lack of strength.** The chances that improper lifting or making a quick move will throw your back out are far greater if your back and abdominal muscles are weak. That's where the strength-training exercises in chapter 9 can help. By strengthening all the muscles that support the spine, you'll reduce your risk of back strain.

- **Too-tight muscles.** Most people, even in their early twenties and thirties, aren't as active as they were in their teens. Becoming less active causes the muscles to stiffen up and become more vulnerable to injury. Whereas supple muscles extend rather easily, tight muscles have such a limited range that even a simple maneuver—picking up a child's toy, for instance, or leaning forward to feed the baby— can trigger a painful pop.

- **Poor posture.** When the shoulders are rounded and the hips thrust forward due to poor posture, they tug on the back muscles, eventually causing both the upper and lower back to ache.

- **Extra weight.** Carrying an excessive number of pounds around, particularly when it's in the abdominal area, increases the curve in the lower back, stretching out the hip flexors and causing the back muscles to tighten up to help stabilize the spine.

By getting in shape, you're taking the most important step possible toward protecting your back. If you do in any case find yourself in pain, the good news is that most people who have acute back pain—pain that lasts a few days or weeks—get better within a few days without the help of a doctor. In the meantime, you can decrease the strain on your back with a few simple stretches. Here are three that may help and can be done several times a day:

Bent-knee stretch

Lie on your back with your knees bent, feet flat on the floor. Raise you knees toward your chest, then place both hands under your knees and gently pull them toward your chest. Keep your head and back on the floor. Hold for 20 to 40 seconds. Repeat four times.

Stomach stretch

Lie on your stomach. Place your hands under your shoulders with your elbows bent and gently push your upper body up. Raise as high as comfortably possible, keeping your hips and legs flat on the floor. Hold for one to two seconds. Repeat nine times.

Backward stretch

Stand with your feet slightly apart with your knees straight. Place your hands in the small of your back and bend backward at your waist as far as comfortably possible. Hold for one to two seconds. Repeat four times.

ten

The Secrets to Sticking With It

YOU'VE PROBABLY HEARD IT BEFORE: "Losing weight is easy. Keeping it off is the hard part." The same thing might be said about exercise. It's easy enough to start an exercise program, but sticking with it is the real challenge. In fact, some experts estimate that at least 50 percent of people who start a physical activity program eventually abandon it.

What makes someone who sets out as an enthusiastic exerciser become a fitness dropout? Researchers have determined that there's not one easy answer. Many people, for instance, stop exercising because of an injury, then never resume exercising. Some people are pressured for time, and feel like something has to give, so they let their workouts go. Others call it quits because they're not getting the results they had hoped to see. Still others simply get bored or become easily distracted by anything else that seems like a more interesting way to spend time.

If you've gone through the stop-and-start routine with exercise before, you probably have a good sense of your own personal pitfalls. This time, instead of waiting until you fall off the wagon, head off any fitness lapses by doing all you can to stay motivated. As much as physical activity involves working the body, it's difficult to keep it up without putting your mind to it, too.

Nobody is perfect and no *body* is always perfectly energetic. There will be times you don't feel like exercising. What's critical, though, is that you don't let a rest day here and there turn into months of inactivity. You may even need to hire a trainer to get back on track or help vary your routine, but remember that you already have a great coach: yourself.

Although family and friends can help you stay motivated, to truly achieve success, you will have to look to yourself for inspiration. You can start by being your own "cheerleader," giving yourself encouragement and thinking positive thoughts. Try and notice the positive results you *are* getting from exercise. Replace negative thinking with positive reinforcement—instead of thinking: "Weight lifting hasn't given me the arms of a supermodel," you'll say "Each week, I'm getting stronger and better looking arms"—and you'll be much more likely to maintain your resolve to exercise.

Ultimately, exercise will become as integral a part of your life as eating and sleeping. Better yet, once it becomes a habit, you'll find it a lot easier to overcome any of the motivational barriers that crop up over time. It also will help if you have some solid strategies to keep you in the right frame of mind.

SETTING GOALS

Even the most diligent person would be hard-pressed to keep exercising if she didn't feel she was getting some sort of payoff for all her hard work. Physical activity should give you a sense of accomplishment, but it's not an instant fix. So, if your goals are unrealistic, you will not only set yourself up for failure, you will probably make yourself miserable.

What's an *unrealistic* goal? The notion that a size-12 body can be exercised into a size-8 body in two weeks; or that a previously sedentary person should be able to walk six miles after a month's training. As you embark upon the **Fit Factor Plan,** make a clear assessment of your exercise level and how quickly you can expect to progress. Be clear about how much weight it's possible to lose within a given amount of time as well. This plan is designed to help you lose weight at a rate of one to two pounds a week—gradually, and at a pace that has been shown to secure better success at keeping lost pounds from creeping back on.

You may find it helpful to write down your goals once a month and compare them to what you've accomplished. If there is a big gap between your aims and your achievements, give your goals a reality check. If your goals are realistic, but you're not meeting them, you may need to tweak your work-out regimen to get better results.

BEING ACCOUNTABLE

Say you decide to work out to a step aerobics video twice a week, walk twice a week, and lift weights twice a week. Then, after some time, you start to slip to the point where you're lucky if you can manage one weekly workout. You feel a little guilty, but nobody knows that you're slacking off, right?

By making a "contract" with a friend or family member, you will have someone to be accountable to—and more incentive to keep exercising. Besides, even if you are your own best coach, it helps to have the support of those you care about. If, however, you feel uncomfortable asking someone to monitor you, try keeping an exercise journal. Reporting to your journal can serve as a daily reminder that you've made a contract with yourself to incorporate exercise into your life. A journal can also give you a way to chart your progress and see the gains you make in black and white.

THREE BARRIERS YOU CAN BEAT

There are always hurdles that get in the way of exercise. Fortunately, there are reasonable ways to get around them, too. Here are some solutions to three of the most common exercise barriers:

Time barrier

You aren't able to get in the hour-long aerobics class you planned and end up having only enough time for a ten-minute walk. Why bother?

Sensible solution: Take the walk. There's nothing more damaging to an exercise program than all-or-nothing thinking. A quick walk might seem hardly worth the bother, but in fact, every little bit of exercise helps. Even ten minutes of walking burns calories and helps maintain fitness, so even if you can't fulfill your original goal, do whatever you can until you get back on track.

If you keep finding yourself in a time crunch, it may be that you need to rethink your exercise schedule. Perhaps evening activity isn't working out because you always end up working too late. You may need to wake up half an hour earlier in the morning to squeeze in exercise. If the reverse is your problem—you end up shutting off the alarm and rolling out of bed too late to work out—maybe you need to set aside part of your lunch hour for activity.

Energy barrier

You're too tired to exercise.

Sensible solution: Give it ten minutes. According to a Greek proverb, "The beginning is the end of every action," and that's definitely true when it comes to exercise. Getting started is particularly hard—the first few minutes of a workout are generally tough. That's because it takes some time for the blood to be shunted away from the organs to your major muscles when you first begin exercising. Once your body is revved up, though, exercise becomes easier and more pleasurable.

With that in mind, make a deal with yourself: On days when you feel too tired to exercise, go out and do it anyway for ten minutes. If you're still feeling fatigued after ten minutes, allow yourself to stop. Chances are, after ten minutes, you'll feel better and amenable to continuing your workout to the end.

Location barrier

You're going on vacation or you travel on business.

Sensible solution: No matter where you go (even if it's a cruise ship), you can always walk. Many hotels also have gyms and equipment to use. You may typically cycle or use a stationary bike, but if you can't participate in your usual activity while you're away, walking makes a great substitute. As for strength training, you may have to take a break from lifting weights if a gym is not accessible. However, you can always do the calisthenics portion of your workout—sit-ups, push-ups, and squats (without holding hand weights). These activities should help keep you in shape while you're away. Also, consider investing in some stretch cords or exercise bands, which are ideal portable tools for resistance exercise. The best solution of all, however, may be to take an active vacation, like a hiking or kayaking trip, or look for an interesting activity if you have time on your business trip.

Most importantly, if you ultimately end up forgoing exercise altogether while you're away, don't use it as an excuse ("I've already blown it!") to break your commitment to physical activity when you return home.

REWARDING YOURSELF

You don't need a lot of equipment to exercise, but using some of the neat gear available as a reward for all your hard work can be fun and motivating. For each 15 minutes you add to your workout, why not treat yourself to a new pair of bicycle shorts, a sports watch, or just a new pair of athletic socks? The rewards don't have to be exercise-related, either. If you've kept up your strength-training routine for a month, celebrate by getting a manicure and pedicure or buying yourself the latest best-seller. Your true reward will be the improvement in how you look and feel, but it doesn't hurt to have some other incentives to help you along the way.

RECOGNIZING RELAPSES

It's not unusual for someone who has been waylaid by an injury, a maddeningly tight schedule, or even a few days or weeks of inactivity, to conclude that she has no willpower. In fact, it can make you feel so bad about yourself that it's hard to get back on track. Whatever you do, don't let a relapse keep you from restarting your exercise program: It's normal for anyone who's making a big change in their lifestyle to suffer through a few setbacks.

The best way to deal with a backslide is to dust yourself off and start again. And stay positive: You may have lost less fitness than you think (see "What Happens When You Slack Off," page 140), and since you already know what to do and how to do it, starting up again shouldn't be too painful. After a break of longer than a week, however, you shouldn't try to start where you left off. Give your body time to build back up to where you were.

What Happens When You Slack Off?

It takes longer to get *out* of shape than it takes to get *in* shape, which means it will probably be a lot less painful to resume exercising after a relapse than you think. Here's a general timetable:

Stopping strength training: On average, most people lose strength at about half the rate they gain it. Thus, if you've been lifting weights for six months, it could be up to a year before you return to your previous state. And there are mitigating factors. If, for instance, you've been lifting multiple sets during each exercise, you're likely to stay stronger, longer, than if you'd only been lifting one or two sets per exercise.

Although it takes two to three strength-training workouts a week to *build* strength, research has shown that even if you cut back your workouts to once a week, you can still *maintain* your strength if you keep intensity constant. The same holds true for aerobic fitness. So, if you find yourself with little time to spare, try to get in at least one strength-training session a week until you can resume your regular workout schedule.

Taking an aerobic hiatus: The fitness effects of aerobic exercise start to decline in about two to three weeks. The rate at which cardiovascular capacity diminishes after that is variable. One study conducted several years ago at the human performance laboratory at the University of Florida, Gainesville, found that runners who'd been training for five months, then took three months off, lost 50 percent of their cardiovascular capacity gains. True, it's a substantial reduction, but the layoff didn't completely wipe out all of the participants' previous hard work. It takes about eight months before you get to that point.

If you've worked out regularly for many months or years before taking a vacation from fitness, you're likely to snap back quicker than if you were just starting from scratch. Although it may vary from person to person, some experts estimate that it takes about half the time to get back into shape. So, if you've taken off a month, give yourself two weeks to regain your former level of fitness, one month if you've taken off two months and so on.

KEEPING IT INTERESTING

Some people like to do the same thing day in and day out. Most people, though, find it tedious—and nothing dampens the incentive to exercise like boredom. Luckily, there are many things you can do to shake up your workouts. Cross training tops the list, so if you're not already varying the types of aerobic exercise you do, start by mixing it up. Then, consider the following options:

- **Alter your routine.** Although strength training is a fairly staid form of exercise, a change of venue might be just what you need to recapture your interest. If you're working out at home, try strength training at a gym. There, you have the option of using free weights or weight machines as well. If you're bored by one, now is a good time to try the other. Or try organizing resistance exercises into an exercise circuit.

- **Change with the seasons.** There's no law that says you have to stick with one type of aerobic exercise all year round. To spice up your routine, try working out in waves by breaking the year up into four segments, according to the seasons. For example, in the winter, work out on the stair climber and stationary bike at the gym; when spring rolls around, head outdoors to walk and cycle; in summer, switch to swimming and hiking; in the fall, in-line skate and use a step aerobics video.

- **Join the club.** There are organized group workouts offered in just about every area of the country, for just about every activity. Work-out groups offer good camaraderie and can help keep you on your toes. You'll be more likely to exercise if you know you'll be missed by the group and, once you arrive for the scheduled activity, you'll probably find that the energy of your exercise mates is contagious.

  Exercise groups also give you the opportunity to trade exercise tips with like-minded people. Some groups even have coaches who can help you improve your workouts and give you the option of training for local, regional, and national competitions. To find a workout group in your area, check local fitness publications, ask at sports stores, search web sites and contact national sports organizations (such as U.S. Masters Swimming or The Road Runners Club of America). If you can't find anything appealing in your area, consider forming your own group.

- **Start training.** All over the country, there are competitions or group exercise events on the calendar. Choosing one of them—anything from a 5-K walk to a 25-mile bicycle ride for charity—will give you a goal to work towards and is a great way to put the strength and endurance you've been building to the test. If you've never thought of yourself as the competitive type, don't be intimidated by the idea of a race. Most big events are designed to get people out to have a healthy dose of fun—the idea isn't to beat someone else as much as it is to go out and achieve your personal best.

A FEW LAST WORDS ON BEING ACTIVE

As you embark on the **Fit Factor Plan,** try to think of yourself as not just an exerciser, but as an active person. Active, in the sense that you move whenever possible; and active, in the sense that you're taking an active role in your health and well-being. Congratulate yourself for stepping up to the challenge. Switching from unhealthy to healthy habits isn't easy, but by swinging into action, you're already on the road to success.

The most difficult part is sticking with your new habits, but recasting the way you think about yourself can help. An active person, for instance, is someone who thinks of exercise as the cure for what ails her. On the mornings when you're so tired that you'd rather roll over and go back to sleep than get up and work out, or on the evenings when you're too tired for a visit to the gym, focus on how good you'll feel after exercising. Likewise, when you're discouraged about your body or stressed out about life's problems, seek relief in a long walk, or spend some time pumping iron. It may take extra energy to get going, but the payoff will make it worthwhile.

An active person is also someone who knows the value of maintaining a nutritious diet. Quite simply, exercise is easier when the body is properly fueled. When you're tempted to dive into the junk food, consider that you're not only diminishing some of your hard work, but making it more difficult for your body to operate in top form. Think of exercise as a tool for helping you subvert the urge to eat, as well. When you're out riding your bike in the neighborhood, or going through the paces on a treadmill, you're a lot less likely to think about food.

Another characteristic of an active person is body confidence. Each time you exercise, even if you're just lifting a few pounds or taking a walk, you are demonstrating that you own a complex and elegant machine. As your body grows stronger, so should your pride in your physical achievements. Granted, by today's cultural standards, it's easy to feel that the only worthy body is super-model thin. The truth is, however, the most desirable body is one that is fit—and one that allows you to go through your day-to-day life with ease and pleasure. Aim not to compare yourself negatively to other people. As an active person, you're striving to have the healthiest and most fit body you can. And, in a world where many people are barely willing to get up to change the channel on the television, that is no small accomplishment.

Part III

FUELING YOURSELF FOR FITNESS

eleven

Nutrition 101 for Exercisers

Exercise and good nutrition are the most effective partners in the weight-loss game. There is no doubt among weight-loss experts that it's more difficult to shed pounds using just one partner and not the other. What's more, study after study has shown that it's nearly impossible to keep off lost weight without combining conscientious eating and regular exercise.

It's also important to combine the two in the interest of maintaining good health. If your goal is to lower your risk of osteoporosis, for example, all the weight-bearing exercise in the world won't keep your bones strong if you're not getting adequate calcium in your diet. Likewise, even if your diet is low in saturated fat and high in soluble fiber—two mainstays of heart-healthy eating—you won't be doing all you can to guard against heart disease unless you include regular cardiovascular workouts into your health regimen.

While the thought of changing both your physical activity level and your eating habits at the same time can be daunting, there really is no better time to rethink your diet than when you're about to embark upon a new exercise program. Eating well is always important, but never more so than when you're asking your body to meet the demands of vigorous exercise. The better the quality of the fuel you take in, the more energy you'll have and the easier your workouts will be.

Profile in Fitness

NAME: DEBBIE B.

OCCUPATION: REALTY SPECIALIST

HOME STATE: LOUISIANA

AGE: 45 YEARS OLD

BEFORE WEIGHT: 244 LBS

AFTER WEIGHT: 135 LBS

HEIGHT: 5'5"

HOW SHE STAYS STRONG AND FIT:

WALKING, $^1/_2$ HOUR AT LUNCH, 2 MILES AFTER WORK

STRENGTH TRAINING, 3 TIMES PER WEEK

*"It all comes down to the way working out
makes me feel. And that's a whole lot better than the
way I felt when I was twenty!"*

I was always overweight. When I quit smoking, I gained even more weight. This past year, I joined Weight Watchers once again, realizing that I was going to be 45 and fat. I couldn't do anything about being my age, but I could do something about my body.

In my entire life, I had never exercised. I received all the Weight Watchers pamphlets on working out, and I thought, "Let me give this a try and see if it works." I took off all the clothes that were hanging on my treadmill for ten years and started walking at the lowest speed. I could only do it for three minutes before I was out of breath. I thought, "Maybe I'll be able do it longer tomorrow." And every day, I did a little more, working up to five minutes. By the end of that first week, I lost close to five pounds.

Every single day, I force myself to work out. I created my own "One-Year Improvement Plan," a weekly record of how much I exercised, the number of POINTS® I used, and how many pounds I lost.

In my previous weight-loss attempts, there would be many weeks when I would plateau, but this time, exercise made all the difference. I didn't need to quit out of frustration, like I had in the past.

It all comes down to the way working out makes me feel. And that's a whole lot better than the way I felt when I was twenty! I was tired all the time and now I'm not. It's like someone gave me a drink from the Fountain of Youth. That's why I know I can't ever give up the exercise— that's the secret to sticking with it.

FROM FOOD TO FUEL

Starting a new work-out program can generally make you feel one of two ways: you're tempted to eat more (and less healthful) foods because you've "earned" the right, or you're inspired to improve your eating habits to build on the benefits you're getting from exercise.

It's easy to see how exercise could make you feel entitled to reward yourself for your hard work. However, you're kidding yourself if you think that you can eat as much of anything you want (including junk food) and still drop pounds or maintain your weight because you exercise.

As you embark on the **Fit Factor Plan**, you should feel inspired to clean up your nutrition act, not clean out your refrigerator. As a regular exerciser, you don't need to follow a special diet, but you do need to be diligent about getting the proper amounts of carbohydrates, protein, fats, and fluids, as well as incorporating certain vitamins and minerals into your eating plan. At the same time, you'll want to make sure that your calorie intake is high enough to help fuel your workouts— but not so high that it prohibits you from losing weight.

If this sounds like a lot to swallow, consider the following information on how your body utilizes fuel. The body relies on three forms of fuel:

- Carbohydrates: primarily from grain-foods, like bread and pasta; fruits and vegetables; and sugars, like table sugar and maple syrup.

- Fat: from oils; animal foods, like butter, milk, and meat; and some fruits, like avocados and olives.

- Protein: primarily from meats, poultry, and fish; legumes (beans and peas); and dairy products.

Although the body uses a very small amount of protein for energy, stored fat and carbohydrates are the muscles' preferred fuel. After your body digests the carbohydrates you eat, it converts them to a simple sugar called glucose. Some of the glucose circulates in your blood, but most of it is converted to a substance called glycogen (actually a long chain of glucose molecules) and is stored in the muscles and liver.

When you exercise—and even when you're at rest—your body uses oxygen to break down glycogen from the muscles and glucose from the blood, fatty acids from stored body fat, and a very small amount of amino acids from protein to produce a substance called adenosine triphosphate (ATP). ATP is a high-energy compound, which ultimately fuels your muscles.

How much your body relies on fat and how much it relies on carbohydrates to produce energy during exercise depends on the intensity and duration of your workouts. During low intensity exercise, the body depends mostly on stored body fat; during exercise that's 60 to 80 percent of maximum heart rate, it depends on fat and carbohydrates about equally. As exercise gets more intense (above 80 percent of maximum heart rate), however, the effort is almost entirely fueled by carbohydrates.

Where does protein fit into the picture? Although it doesn't figure greatly into energy metabolism, protein still plays an important role in an exerciser's diet. Protein helps maintain, build, and repair muscles, insuring that muscle tissue broken down and/or stimulated to grow during strength training rebuilds itself. Also, protein is used to make hemoglobin (the component of blood responsible for transporting oxygen to exercising muscles), and produce enzymes and hormones that regulate all body processes.

THE PERFECT BALANCE

Exercise helps you lose weight precisely because it makes you burn *more* fat and carbohydrates than you consume. It doesn't, however, significantly alter the ratio of these nutrients: you need a diet that's 50 to 60 percent carbohydrates (preferably the unrefined, complex variety) and 20 to 30 percent fat (preferably unsaturated fatty acids), with protein making up the difference.

The *type* of carbohydrates, fat, and protein you eat counts, too. When you make your food choices, keep the following information in mind.

Carbohydrates

There are two different types of carbohydrates: simple and complex. Simple carbohydrates, such as those in sugar, honey, syrup, and the sugar in fruit and fruit juice, are easily converted by the body to blood glucose, which can then be used by the muscles and the brain for energy. The trouble with most simple carbohydrate foods is that they have very few nutrients. They're not "bad" for you, but eating too many simple carbohydrates (particularly in the form of table sugar and the hidden sugars in cakes, soda, jams, etc.) may not leave room for foods that have the vitamins, minerals, and fiber you need.

Unprocessed complex carbohydrates, on the other hand, are generally nutrient-dense and fiber-rich. The prime sources of complex carbohydrates are starchy foods, like cereals, potatoes, brown rice, bread, and pasta, and vegetables and fruits (fruits have both simple and complex carbohydrates). Beans, although generally considered a protein food, also contain complex carbohydrates.

One of the most important components of unrefined complex carbohydrates—those which are digested and absorbed more slowly by the body, preventing less dramatic swings in blood glucose—is fiber. Fiber comes in two forms, soluble and insoluble. Soluble fiber, found primarily in oat bran, barley, fruit, carrots, and legumes, has been shown to help lower blood cholesterol. Insoluble fiber, found in whole grains, wheat bran, and the skin of fruits and vegetables, may help protect against colon cancer and other gastrointestinal disorders by increasing elimination of waste through the digestive tract. Some evidence also suggests that a diet high in fiber may help deter breast cancer by altering hormone levels, as well as decrease the risk of diabetes.

Although many people eat plenty of grain products, nutrition experts lament that they don't eat more *whole*-grain products, a prime source of fiber. Bulking up the diet with foods like whole-wheat bread, cereals made from whole grains (like oatmeal), and whole-wheat pastas, makes it easier to meet the daily recommendation of 25 to 35 grams of fiber. Better yet, whole-grain foods, in particular, have been linked to disease prevention: According to recent data from the Harvard Nurses' Study, women who make whole grains a substantial part of their diet have a lower risk of heart disease.

Fats

Ounce per ounce, fat has more calories than either carbohydrates or protein (nine calories per gram of fat; four calories per gram of both proteins and carbohydrates), one of several reasons it makes sense to maintain a low-fat diet. However, it's important to realize that although fat has been vilified, it actually has a place in a healthy diet. Without adequate fat, your body would have trouble making hormones and absorbing the fat-soluble vitamins A, D, E, and K. Some fats, eaten in moderation, can even lower your risk of disease. For instance, monounsaturated fats, found in olive and canola oils, reduce LDL (the "bad") cholesterol levels in the blood without lowering HDL (the "good") cholesterol levels, thus lowering the likelihood of heart disease. Omega-3 fatty acids, found primarily in fish, also reduce the risk of heart disease, and linolenic acid, a fat contained in flaxseeds, soybeans, and walnuts, has been associated with a reduced risk of cancer.

When eaten in excess, some fats have the opposite effect. These fats, like saturated fat and hydrogenated fat, raise blood cholesterol levels—even more than dietary cholesterol—and increase the risk of heart disease and cancer. Saturated fats are found in animal foods like meats and dairy products, and in palm and coconut oils. Hydrogenation, which involves adding hydrogen to a fat's chemical makeup, is used to turn liquid fats into solids. Margarine is a hydrogenated fat, as are many of the fats used in baked goods.

Even though exercisers are less likely to suffer from heart disease than nonexercisers, working out can't make you immune to the effects of a diet high in saturated fat. So, while keeping your overall fat intake in the 20 to 30 percent of total calories range, you should also limit your intake of saturated fats to no more than ten percent of your daily calories. The American Heart Association Step II Diet for people who already have heart disease, even calls for lowering saturated fat to seven percent of total calories.

Protein

Most Americans get more than their fair share of protein, and these days, some exercisers are consuming even larger quantities of the nutrient in a misguided effort to bolster their workouts. Certainly, active people need to be especially protein-conscious because they depend on the nutrient for the building and repair of muscle tissue. (Protein also helps maintain infection-fighting antibodies in the blood, critical enzymes, and healthy hair and nails.) Nonetheless, the average exerciser doesn't need more than about 0.8 grams of protein per every 2.2 pounds of body weight, or if you weigh 150 pounds, you require about 55 grams daily. Be warned: Consuming too much protein can put you at risk for dehydration since excess protein makes the body excrete water. It can also cause the body to excrete calcium, thus increasing the risk of osteoporosis.

On the other hand, some individuals shun protein foods since they often come hand in hand with fat—the best example is a thick, juicy steak. In reality, most sources of protein are fairly lean. Some of the best choices are skim milk, nonfat yogurt, nonfat cottage cheese, egg whites, white meat poultry, fish and shellfish, tofu, and legumes.

FACTS ON VITAMINS AND MINERALS

A common misconception is that vitamins and minerals provide energy. In fact, they aren't sources of energy themselves, but they do play a large role in the release of energy. You wouldn't have the stamina to exercise without them.

Although each vitamin and mineral has its own unique function, vitamins, in general, facilitate every chemical reaction in the body. Minerals are responsible for regulating the body's enzymes, fluid balance, muscle contractions, and nerve transmissions.

In order to accomplish these tasks, the body doesn't need large quantities of vitamins and minerals but, rather, a supply that is constantly replenished. With that in mind, the Food and Nutrition Board of the National Research Council/National Academy of Science established the Recommended Dietary Allowances (RDAs) in 1943, and continually reassess these numbers as new research develops.

Iron and Exercise

One of the roles of the mineral, iron, is to transport oxygen to the working muscles. Without proper iron reserves, you may feel fatigued while exercising. In fact, an estimated 30 to 50 percent of women are iron-deficient, particularly around the time of menstruation when iron losses can range between 5 and 45 milligrams. Some researchers believe that women who exercise heavily may be at greater risk for an iron deficiency, since intense activity may tap out the body's iron reserves. However, the general belief is that increased physical activity places a woman at no greater risk for iron deficiencies than the risk for women, in general.

The best dietary sources of iron are red meat and liver, seafood, legumes, dark leafy greens, and fortified breads and cereals. The iron in animal foods, called heme iron, is better absorbed by the body (10 to 35 percent) than the iron in vegetarian sources (only 2 to 10 percent), called nonheme iron. It may, therefore, be more difficult for vegetarians or people trying to cut back on meat, to get adequate iron. Those individuals can increase the absorption of nonheme iron by eating it together with foods rich in vitamin C. For instance, drinking a glass of orange juice with breakfast will help you absorb three times the amount of iron from a meal than you would without a C-source.

The RDAs are the daily amounts of different food nutrients needed for healthy individuals.

There aren't different RDAs for exercisers and, in general, you don't need more vitamins and minerals even if you're working out vigorously. But there are a few vitamins and minerals that may deserve more of your attention:

- **Calcium.** Exercise will help strengthen your bones, thus lowering your risk of osteoporosis, but you still need to have an adequate intake of calcium. Calcium is necessary not only for the health of your bones and teeth, but for physical activity because of it's instrumental role in the conversion of food to energy. Calcium, which is involved in the nerve-muscle connection, also insures that your muscles contract when you demand it.

- **B vitamins.** It's especially important for active women to get enough B vitamins—thiamin, riboflavin, vitamin B-6, pantothenic acid, folic acid, vitamin B-12, biotin, and niacin. The B vitamins' main job is to team up with enzymes to break down carbohydrates, fat, and protein into fuel that can then be used to make ATP (see page 150). There's some evidence that exercise increases the turnover of B vitamins, so exercisers should be especially diligent about meeting their B-related RDAs.

- **Vitamins E and C.** Both vitamin E and vitamin C are antioxidant vitamins, a class of vitamins that help prevent the actions of free radicals, the maverick molecules with at least one unpaired electron that cause damage to healthy cells. One by-product of vigorous exercise is an increased production of free radicals, which can cause muscle soreness. While a well-nourished body can generally defend itself against the errant molecules, one that is deficient in vitamin E and vitamin C may have more trouble, since these antioxidants help repair the tiny tears in muscles responsible for post-workout pain. Studies have shown that exercisers who take vitamin E and vitamin C supplements have less muscle soreness than those who take placebos.

Does this mean you should supplement your diet? Probably not. The outcomes of these studies are still preliminary and the subjects are generally athletes who exercise at high levels. The best way to make sure you meet your RDAs is to eat a varied diet and, in particular, a variety of fruits and vegetables: Produce is one of the best sources of vitamins and minerals. In addition, fruits and vegetables are rich in phytochemicals, plant chemicals that stimulate natural detoxifying enzymes in the body and have a protective effect against cancer. Some of the most reliable data available on disease prevention indicates that people who eat a lot of fruits and vegetables live longer.

While you may want to make a special effort to get calcium, B vitamins, vitamin E, and vitamin C, your best course of action is still to concentrate on getting a wide variety of nutrients in your diet. The following chart will help give you an idea of what you need, why you need it, and how to make sure that you get it. (You'll notice that

VITAMINS	WHAT THEY DO	BEST SOURCES
Vitamins (Water-Soluble) Thiamin (Vitamin B1)	Instrumental in the breakdown of carbo-hydrates. Promotes normal appetite, digestion, and proper nerve function.	Fortified grains/cereals. Whole grains. Nuts. Milk. Legumes. Seafood. Pork.
Riboflavin (Vitamin B2)	Aids in the metabolism of all foods and the release of energy to cells. Maintains mucous membranes. Helps maintain vision.	Meats. Eggs. Dairy products. Fortified grains/cereals. Whole grains. Green leafy vegetables.
Niacin (Vitamin B3)	Plays a role in converting fats and carbohydrates to energy. Promotes normal appetite, digestion, and proper nerve function.	Meats. Poultry. Whole grains. Legumes. Peanuts. Liver.
Pyroxidine (Vitamin B6)	Essential to protein and carbohydrate metabolism. Helps form red blood cells and promotes proper nerve function.	Beef. Pork. Poultry. Fish (especially tuna and salmon). Whole grains. Fortified grains/cereals. Seeds. Baked potato skins. Avocados. Sweet potatoes. Spinach. Prunes.
Pantothenic acid (Vitamin B5)	Helps convert food to molecular forms needed for energy. Aids in the manu-facture of adrenal hormones and nerve regulation.	Manufactured by intestinal bacteria. Also in most foods, including meats, fish, poultry, dairy prod-ucts, legumes, whole grains.
Folic Acid	Needed to make genetic material and to manufac-ture red blood cells.	Legumes. Green veg-etables such as spinach, asparagus, and broccoli. Oatmeal. Whole-wheat products. Fortified grains/cereals. Eggs. Dairy products. Liver. Orange and grapefruit juice.
Cobalamin (Vitamin B12)	Builds genetic material and helps manufacture red blood cells.	All animal products, including meats, poultry, seafood, eggs. Dairy products.

VITAMINS	WHAT THEY DO	BEST SOURCES
Biotin	Aids in the metabolism of glucose and amino acids and the formation of fatty acids.	Manufactured by intestinal bacteria. Also: Legumes. Meat. Liver. Egg yolks. Nuts.
Vitamin C	Helps maintain cartilage and bone. Binds cells together and strengthens blood vessel walls. Aids in infection-resistance and the healing of cuts and wounds.	Citrus fruits. Strawberries. Red and green peppers. Broccoli. Brussels sprouts. Papaya. Cantaloupe. Sweet potatoes. Cabbage.
Vitamins (Fat-Soluble) Vitamin A	Keeps skin, hair, and nails healthy. Maintains gums, glands, bones, teeth. Helps prevent infection and promotes eye function.	Dairy products. Fortified cereals. Organ meats.
Beta Carotene (Converted into vitamin A by the body)	All of the above. Functions as an antioxidant to help prevent cell damage. May help protect against cancer.	Leafy green vegetables like collard greens, kale, spinach. Orange vegetables such as sweet potatoes, pumpkin, winter squash, carrots. Mango. Cantaloupe.
Vitamin D	Promotes growth and mineralization of the teeth and bones. Assists the body in absorbing calcium.	Egg yolks. Fish. Fortified milk and butter. Manufactured by the body with exposure to the sun.
Vitamin E	Functions as an antioxidant to help prevent cell damage. Helps form red blood cells, muscles, and other tissues.	Poultry. Seafood. Seeds. Nuts. Cooked greens. Wheat germ. Fortified cereals. Eggs.
Vitamin K	Important in blood clotting.	Manufactured by intestinal bacteria. Green leafy vegetables like spinach. Oats, wheat bran, and other whole grains. Potatoes. Cabbage. Organ meats.

MINERALS	WHAT THEY DO	BEST SOURCES
Minerals (macrominerals)		
Calcium	Helps build strong bones and teeth. Promotes proper muscle and nerve function. Aids in blood clotting. Activates enzymes needed to convert food to energy.	Dairy products. Canned sardines and salmon with bones. Green leafy vegetables. Broccoli. Tofu.
Phosphorous	Works with calcium to build and maintain bones and teeth. Helps convert food to energy and maintain proper nerve and muscle function.	Dairy products. Egg yolks. Meat. Poultry. Fish. Legumes.
Magnesium	Activates enzymes needed to synthesize protein. Promotes bone growth. Instrumental in making cells and genetic material.	Whole grains like brown rice. Green leafy vegetables such as spinach and Swiss chard. Legumes. Almonds. Fortified breads/cereals. Fish.
Potassium	Helps regulate fluid balance. Promotes transmission of nerve impulses and muscle contractions.	Bananas. Citrus fruits. Dried fruits. Green leafy vegetables such as beet greens. Potato with skin. Clams. Avocado. Legumes. Fish.
Sodium	Aids in the maintenance of body fluid balance and nerve function.	Salt. Processed foods. Milk. Drinking water.
Chloride	Helps maintain fluid balance outside the cells.	Salt. Processed foods. Milk. Drinking water.
Minerals (trace)		
Iron	Integral to making hemoglobin, which carries oxygen in blood. Helps create enzymes involved in metabolizing food.	Red meat. Liver. Seafood. Legumes. Dried apricots. Fortified breads/cereals. Acidic foods cooked in cast-iron pots.
Zinc	Helps produce enzymes involved in digestion.	Oysters. Meat. Poultry. Legumes. Nuts. Wheat germ. Fortified cereals.

MINERALS	WHAT THEY DO	BEST SOURCES
Selenium	Interacts with vitamin E to prevent breakdown of fats and body chemicals	Brazil nuts. Canned tuna. Oysters. Poultry. Whole grains. Eggs. Mushrooms. Onions. Garlic.
Copper	Involved in the production of enzymes associated with protein metabolism.	Meat. Drinking water. Lobster. Nuts. Legumes. Barley. Prunes.
Iodine	Essential to normal function of the thyroid gland.	Seafood. Iodized salt.
Fluoride	Promotes strong bones and teeth. Improves the uptake of calcium.	Fluoridated water. Tea. Seafood.
Chromium	Works with insulin for proper glucose metabolism.	Whole-grain breads and cereals. Brewer's yeast. Peanuts. Organ meats.
Sulfur	Needed to make hair and nails. Aids in liver function.	Wheat germ. Dried pasta. Legumes. Beef. Peanuts. Clams.

vitamins fall into two categories: water-soluble and fat-soluble. It's difficult to overdose on water-soluble vitamins since any excess is flushed out of the body; fat-soluble vitamins, however, get stored in body fat and tend to accumulate, so getting too much of some fat-soluble vitamins can be dangerous.)

OF WATER, BREAKFAST, AND SNACKS

Even if you're well versed about the important role good nutrition plays in terms of exercise, you still may find yourself falling prey to common dietary pitfalls. Here, three key areas that seem to continually pop up for women trying to get a handle on the ABCs of eating right.

Water and your wellness

Water makes up 40 to 60 percent of your body—and you can't live without it. You also can't exercise proficiently without replacing the water you lose during your workouts. During aerobic exercise, it's possible to forfeit as much as one to one and a half quarts of fluid by a combination of sweating and release of moisture through your mouth as you exhale.

The body relies on water to transport everything from nutrients to waste products. Water also helps protect the organs and lubricate the joints and is critical for regulating body temperature. When you're out in hot weather or when you generate extra body heat by exercising, water keeps you from overheating. Its thermostat control role is especially important when your body is faced with a double whammy: exercise in hot weather. So, it's crucial to drink even more water when working out on summer days, particularly if it's humid. The skin is cooled off not by the actual action of sweating, but by the evaporation of sweat from the skin. Since little evaporation takes place when humidity is high, the body has to work harder to cool itself and may eventually become dehydrated.

Dehydration can be serious: Even losing one percent of your body weight in fluid can place strain on your cardiovascular system. Dehydration also limits the body's ability to transfer heat from your working muscles to the skin where it can be dissipated. That can lead to a rapid pulse, headache, nausea, dizziness, and weakness. At its most serious, it can even cause collapse and damage to the nervous system and organs (heat stroke).

Water, of course, isn't the only fluid that helps keep the body hydrated, but it has the added advantage of being calorie-free while making you feel full. Drink plenty of water and you may even eat less. Here's what other beverages have to offer:

- **Juice, sodas.** Both of these drinks provide some hydration, but it may not be a good idea to drink either one before exercise: Their high sugar content can cause stomach distress during a workout. There are also the calories to consider. Juice and sodas both have about 100 calories per cup. And while juice comes with some important nutrients, sodas have nothing to offer but sugar (diet sodas have nothing to offer period).

- **Caffeinated drinks.** Because caffeine is a diuretic—which increases urination—colas, coffee, and tea are actually more dehydrating than hydrating. (Decaffeinated coffee, tea, and colas, and herbals tea are exceptions.) Some studies have shown that caffeine can improve endurance performance, but for the average exerciser who isn't concerned with competition or prolonged exercise, its dehydrating dangers outweigh its benefits.

- **Sports drinks.** These beverages are usually swigged during and after exercise. The advantage of sports drinks is that they not only replace fluids lost through exercise, they replace carbohydrates (in the form of sugar) and electrolytes. Electrolytes—the minerals, sodium, potassium, and chloride—help moderate fluid exchange within the body. Although it certainly won't hurt to sip a sports drink during or after your workout, it's not really necessary, unless you've been exercising for over an hour. And to avoid the extra calories (about 40 per cup), you may want to stick to water.

Drink Up!

Whether you're exercising or not, you should drink six to eight cups of water daily. When you exercise, though, you'll need still more. Here are some guidelines to go by:

- Drink approximately two cups of water in the two hours preceding exercise, then two cups about 15 minutes before your activity.

- As you exercise, drink about one-half cup every 15 minutes.

- After your workout, drink at least two cups of water, and more if you've exercised for over an hour.

Easy Morning Meals

Try to eat at least an hour before you're going to exercise and limit your breakfast to approximately 300 high-carbohydrate calories. Some options:

- 1 cup raisin bran, 1 cup 1-percent milk, $1/2$ banana

- 2 slices whole-wheat toast, 2 teaspoons margarine, 1 cup orange juice

- 1 cup vanilla nonfat yogurt, $1/2$ bagel

- 1 cup oatmeal, $1/3$ cup 1-percent milk, $1/4$ cup raisins

- Small bagel with 1 tablespoon peanut butter

If you don't have time to sit down to a meal an hour before you exercise, you should, at least, drink a glass of juice or eat half of a piece of toast.

Breakfast of exercise champions

Some people simply aren't hungry first thing in the morning. Others don't make the time to eat. But breakfast might just be the most important meal of the day, especially if you're going to be exercising first thing.

After a night's slumber, your body is like a car slogging along on gas fumes—you may be okay for the first few miles, but you probably don't have enough fuel to go the distance. The fuel, in this case, is glucose (and glycogen). When you go more than several hours without eating (e.g., after a night's sleep), the body's supply of blood glucose plummets, as does the large supply of glucose stored as glycogen in the liver and muscles—that leaves you without a good source of quick energy.

Snacking, pre-workout

Eating too close to exercise can make you feel uncomfortable as you work out and even give you stomach cramps. However, you won't be able to perform your best without being well-fueled. If there is a gap of several hours between your last meal and your work-out time, try to eat a light snack about an hour to an hour and a half before exercising (experiment to see how close to your work-out time you feel comfortable eating). When you choose a snack, go for something high in carbohydrates, but avoid very high-fiber foods, like bran and high-fiber cereals, and very salty, sugary, or spicy snacks. Also, steer clear of beans, onions, and broccoli, which can cause intestinal gas.

A Stack of Good Snacks

Here are a few sensible pre-exercise snacks to try:

- 1 low-fat energy bar
- 1 banana
- 1 small, low-fat muffin
- 1 cup tomato soup
- 7 fat-free crackers
- 2 fig bars
- $\frac{1}{2}$ baked sweet potato
- 15 small unsalted pretzels
- 4 graham cracker squares
- $\frac{1}{4}$ cup raisins
- 1 mini bagel
- $\frac{1}{2}$ cup of cereal squares
- 7 small, flavored mini rice cakes

twelve

Good Nutrition in Play

IF YOU'RE READY TO GET SERIOUS ABOUT LOSING WEIGHT and improving your overall health, there's no better way to reap the benefits of a new lifestyle than to adjust your diet, along with making exercise a part of your life. If you're following **Weight Watchers 1•2•3 Success®** plan, our four-week menu (designed for a 150-pound woman) is an effortless way to stick to the Plan. If you're not familiar with the Plan, you may be puzzled by the *POINTS* in the following menus. All foods have a *POINTS* value on the **1•2•3 Success Plan** and every individual is allotted a certain range of *POINTS* each day, depending on her current weight. You may want to consider visiting your nearest Weight Watchers location to learn more about the specifics. In the meantime, the following menu is a great way to sample the merchandise, and start making strides toward a stronger and slimmer you!

WEEK 1

MONDAY

Breakfast

1 whole grain waffle with 1 tablespoon maple syrup (4)
Peachy Smoothie (In a blender, puree 1 peach, $1/2$ banana, $1/2$ cup fat-free milk, $1/2$ cup peach nonfat yogurt, 1 tablespoon wheat germ, and 1 tablespoon bran.) (4.5)
8.5 *POINTS*

Lunch

2 slices high-fiber bread (2)
2 ounces turkey (2)
2 teaspoons mustard
1 cup lettuce leaves, tomato, and red onion slices (0)
1 cup fat-free milk (2)
1 McIntosh apple (1)
7 *POINTS*

Dinner

1 cup borscht with 1 tablespoon nonfat sour cream (2)
4 frozen potato pancakes, heated according to package instructions, with $1/2$ cup applesauce (4.5)
6.5 *POINTS*

Snack

1 pear (1)
3 cups light microwave popcorn (1)
2 *POINTS*

TOTAL FOR THE DAY: 24 *POINTS*

TUESDAY

Breakfast

1 cup wheat flake cereal with 1 cup fat-free milk (3)
3/4 ounce raisins (1)
1/2 grapefruit (1)
5 *POINTS*

Lunch

1 cup tossed salad with 1/2 cup each tomato and cucumber slices,
2 tablespoons fat-free Dijon dressing (1)
2 slices pumpernickel bread (4)
Beef and Horseradish (In a small bowl, mix 1 teaspoon horseradish
with 2 teaspoons fat-free mayonnaise and 1 teaspoon nonfat sour
cream; serve with 2 ounces lean roast beef.) (3)
8 *POINTS*

Dinner

Lemon-Cumin Sole (Sauté 1/2 cup each onions and cilantro,
1 teaspoon garlic, 2 teaspoons cumin, and 1/4 cup lemon juice in
1 tablespoon butter. Spoon over a 3-ounce piece of sole; bake at
375°F for 20 minutes.) (4)
1 cup fat-free milk (2)
1/2 cup cooked brown rice (2)
1 cup steamed spinach (0)
8 *POINTS*

Snack

1 cup watermelon with 1/3 cup cottage cheese (2)
2 *POINTS*

TOTAL FOR THE DAY: 23 *POINTS*

WEDNESDAY

Breakfast

1 egg, scrambled with nonstick cooking spray (2)
1 slice high-fiber wheat toast with 1 teaspoon butter (2)
1 cup fat-free milk (2)
Orange Spritzer (Mix 4 ounces orange juice and 4 ounces seltzer in glass; pour over ice.) (1)
7 *POINTS*

Lunch

1 cup lentil soup (3)
2 cups romaine lettuce with 2 tablespoons fat-free Caesar dressing and Homemade Croutons (Cut 1 slice high-fiber bread into squares; sauté in 1 teaspoon oil; sprinkle with 1/2 teaspoon each garlic powder and parsley.) (3)
1/2 cup each raspberries and blackberries with 1/2 cup lemon sorbet (3)
9 *POINTS*

Dinner

Teriyaki Salmon (Marinate a 3-ounce piece of salmon in a mix of 1 tablespoon each teriyaki sauce and orange juice, and 2 teaspoons shredded gingerroot; about 1 hour. Grill, until cooked through, about 8 minutes.) (2)
1/2 cup brown rice (2)
1 cup steamed broccoli with 1 teaspoon each butter and lemon juice (1)
1 cup fat-free milk (2)
7 *POINTS*

Snack

Grown-Up S'mores (Top 1 scoop [1/2 cup] vanilla fat-free frozen yogurt with 1 teaspoon chocolate sauce and 2 teaspoons flaked coconut; layer between 2 graham crackers.) (3)
3 *POINTS*

TOTAL FOR THE DAY: 26 *POINTS*

THURSDAY

Breakfast

Hiker's Breakfast (Combine $^1/_2$ cup low-fat granola, 1 cup plain non-fat yogurt, and 1 chopped Granny Smith apple.) (6)
6 *POINTS*

Lunch

Shrimp Wrap (Combine 1 cup cooked shrimp with 2 teaspoons reduced-fat mayonnaise and 1 cup alfalfa sprouts; wrap in a 6-inch flour tortilla.) (5)
Carrot-Raisin Salad (Toss together 1 shredded carrot, $^3/_4$ ounce raisins, 1 tablespoon fat-free mayonnaise, and 2 teaspoons lemon juice.) (1)
1 orange (1)
7 *POINTS*

Dinner

Super Burger (Layer one vegetarian burger, lettuce leaves, tomato slices, and 1 teaspoon chili sauce on a high-fiber whole-grain bun.) (4)
Cheese Fries (Toss 1 large, thinly-sliced potato with 1 teaspoon oil; spread on a baking sheet and bake at 400°F until easily pierced with a fork, about 35 minutes. In the microwave, melt $^3/_4$ ounce low-fat cheddar cheese; drizzle over the fries. Sprinkle with salt, to taste, and serve with 2 tablespoons ketchup.) (6)
10 *POINTS*

Snack

1 cup fat-free milk (2)
2 plums (1)
3 *POINTS*

TOTAL FOR THE DAY: 26 *POINTS*

FRIDAY

Breakfast

1 small pumpernickel bagel (3)
1 tablespoon nonfat cream cheese (0)
$^1/_2$ cup each strawberries and blueberries (1)
Malted Latte (Stir together $^1/_2$ cup strong coffee, 1 cup fat-free milk, and 2 teaspoons malt.) (3)
7 *POINTS*

Lunch

Caribbean Cottage Cheese Platter (Top 1 cup mixed greens with $^1/_3$ cup cottage cheese and $^1/_3$ cup each diced mango, pineapple, and papaya; toss with 1 tablespoon each orange juice, rice wine vinegar, and coconut milk.) (3)
1 small fat-free banana muffin (2)
5 *POINTS*

Dinner

2 cups chicory with 2 tablespoons fat-free French dressing (1)
1 4-ounce lobster tail with 1 tablespoon drawn butter and lemon wedges (5)
1 large baked potato (3)
$^1/_2$ cup each steamed zucchini and squash (0)
9 *POINTS*

Snack

12 tortilla chips with $^1/_2$ cup pico de gallo (3)
3 *POINTS*

TOTAL FOR THE DAY: 24 *POINTS*

SATURDAY

Breakfast

2 whole-grain pancakes with 1 teaspoon butter and 1 tablespoon maple syrup (6)

Melon Sunrise (1/3 cup each honeydew, cantaloupe, and watermelon, cut into chunks and sprinkled with lime juice.) (1)

7 *POINTS*

Lunch

Grilled Chicken Salad (Toss 3 cups mixed greens with 1/2 cup each chopped tomatoes and red peppers, 3 ounces grilled chicken breast, 3/4 ounce low-fat cheddar cheese, and 2 tablespoons fat-free Italian dressing.) (5)

1 high-fiber whole grain roll (2)

1 cup aspartame-sweetened strawberry-banana nonfat yogurt (2)

9 *POINTS*

Dinner

5 ounces frozen eggplant Parmesan, prepared according to package directions (3)

1 cup whole wheat spaghetti (3)

6 *POINTS*

Snack

1 rice cake topped with 1 tablespoon peanut butter and 1/2 sliced peach (3)

1 cup fat-free milk (2)

5 *POINTS*

TOTAL FOR THE DAY: 27 *POINTS*

SUNDAY

Breakfast

Broccoli-Cheddar Omelet (Whisk together 1 egg, 2 tablespoons fat-free milk, and 1 tablespoon flour; cook in 1 teaspoon butter, turning once. Sprinkle one half omelet with $3/4$ ounce low-fat cheddar cheese and $1/2$ cup broccoli; fold in half, and sprinkle with salt, to taste.) (5)
Cappuccino made with 1 cup fat-free milk (2)
Mimosa (Mix $1/2$ cup orange juice and $1/2$ cup champagne; serve in a champagne flute.) (3)
10 *POINTS*

Lunch

Goat Cheese Salad (Toss together 3 cups romaine lettuce, $1/2$ cup chopped tomatoes, 3 slices Bermuda onion, and 1 ounce goat cheese; top with homemade croutons (see recipe, Wednesday, Week 1, lunch), and drizzle with 1 tablespoon fat-free red wine vinaigrette.) (5)
5 *POINTS*

Dinner

1 slice meatloaf with $1/4$ cup mushroom gravy (9)
1 cup fat-free milk (2)
1 cup steamed string beans (0)
11 *POINTS*

Snack

1 cup frozen seedless grapes (1)
1 *POINT*

TOTAL FOR THE DAY: 27 *POINTS*

WEEK 2

MONDAY

Breakfast

Banana Oatmeal (Stir together 1 tablespoon wheat germ, 1 tablespoon bran, 1 cup cooked oatmeal, and 1 cup fat-free milk; top with 1 sliced banana and 1 teaspoon brown sugar.) (6)
6 *POINTS*

Lunch

Open-Face Tuna Melt (Mix 4 ounces water-packed tuna and 1 tablespoon fat-free mayonnaise; spoon onto 1 slice high-fiber bread. Top with $^3/_4$ ounce low-fat cheddar cheese and broil until cheese is melted.) (6)
1 cup lemon yogurt (3)
9 *POINTS*

Dinner

Black Bean and Corn Burrito (Layer a 6-inch flour tortilla with 2 ounces cooked black beans, $^1/_4$ cup fresh corn kernels, 2 tablespoons salsa, and $^3/_4$ ounce low-fat Monterey Jack cheese; top with 1 tablespoon fat-free sour cream.) (5)
$^1/_4$ cup guacamole (2)
$^1/_3$ cup each steamed zucchini, red peppers, and onions (0)
7 *POINTS*

Snack

$^1/_2$ cup each orange and grapefruit sections (1)
2 graham crackers (1)
2 *POINTS*

TOTAL FOR THE DAY: 24 *POINTS*

TUESDAY

Breakfast

Yogurt-Granola Parfait (In a tall glass, layer 1 cup aspartame-sweetened blueberry nonfat yogurt, $1/2$ cup low-fat granola, and 1 cup sliced strawberries.) (6)
6 POINTS

Lunch

2 cups green salad with 2 tablespoons fat-free Italian dressing (0)
1 slice cheese pizza (9)
1 apple (1)
10 POINTS

Dinner

Scallop Stir-Fry (Stir-fry 2 ounces scallops in 1 teaspoon oil; add 1 tablespoon hoisin sauce and 1 cup fresh pea pods and cook until pea pods are tender, about 3 minutes.) (2)
1 cup wild rice (3)
$1/2$ cup each carrots and jicama, julienned (0)
5 POINTS

Snack

2 oatmeal-raisin cookies (3)
1 cup fat-free milk (2)
5 POINTS

TOTAL FOR THE DAY: 26 POINTS

WEDNESDAY

Breakfast

Scallion Pancake (Whisk together 1 egg, 2 tablespoons fat-free milk,
1 tablespoon flour, and 1 chopped scallion; cook egg mixture in
1 teaspoon butter, turning once.) (3)
Madras Spritzer (Mix 2 ounces each orange juice and cranberry
juice with 6 ounces seltzer and a spritz of lime in a tall glass.) (1)
4 *POINTS*

Lunch

Turkey On Rye (On 2 slices rye bread, layer 2 ounces sliced turkey,
³/₄ ounce low-fat Swiss cheese, and 1 tablespoon fat-free Thousand
Island dressing.) (9)
¹/₃ cup each yellow, red, and green pepper slices (0)
1 cup fat-free milk (2)
11 *POINTS*

Dinner

Spinach Salad (Toss together 3 cups baby spinach, 1 chopped
tomato, ¹/₂ cup Bermuda onion slices, ¹/₂ cup each cucumber and
red pepper slices, 2 slices crisp-cooked bacon, and 2 tablespoons
fat-free vinaigrette.) (3)
1 small high-fiber whole wheat roll (2)
1 cup aspartame-sweetened nonfat blackberry yogurt (2)
7 *POINTS*

Snack

¹/₂ large sesame bagel with ¹/₂ tablespoon peanut butter (4)
4 *POINTS*

TOTAL FOR THE DAY: 26 *POINTS*

THURSDAY

Breakfast

1 cup bran cereal with 6 chopped dried apricots halves and 1 cup
fat-free milk (4)
4 POINTS

Lunch

Miso Soup (Dissolve 1 tablespoon miso paste in 1 cup water over
medium heat; stir in 1 chopped scallion.) (1)
8 pieces sushi maki (2)
1 cup pineapple chunks (1)
1 cup nonfat calcium-fortified vanilla soy milk (2)
6 POINTS

Dinner

Chicken and Black-Eyed Peas (Brown a 3-ounce skinless chicken
thigh coated with bread crumbs in 2 teaspoons of oil; set aside.
Sauté $^1/_4$ cup each chopped onions, mushrooms, tomatoes, and carrots in 2 teaspoons oil [add a small amount of white wine, if more
liquid is needed]; add 2 ounces cooked black-eyed peas and sea-
soned salt, to taste. Transfer to baking pan, top with the chicken
and bake at 350°F, about 30 minutes. (8)
1 cup steamed green beans (0)
$^1/_2$ cup passion fruit sorbet (2)
10 POINTS

Snack

$^1/_3$ cup each red pepper, carrot, and zucchini sticks
Yogurt-Dill Dip (Mix $^1/_4$ cup plain nonfat yogurt, $^1/_4$ teaspoon
snipped dill, $^1/_4$ teaspoon garlic powder, and 1 teaspoon lemon
juice.) (1)
1 POINT

TOTAL FOR THE DAY: 21 POINTS

FRIDAY

Breakfast

1 small fat-free corn muffin (2)

Mango Madness (In a blender, puree $^1/_2$ mango, $^1/_2$ cup low-fat plain yogurt, and $^1/_2$ cup fat-free milk.) (4)

6 *POINTS*

Lunch

Lamb Gyro (Layer 2 ounces cooked lamb, $^1/_2$ cup each chopped lettuce and tomatoes, $^1/_4$ cup low-fat plain yogurt, and $^1/_2$ cup diced cucumbers on a large pocketless pita; fold over.) (6)

1 cup fat-free milk (2)

8 *POINTS*

Dinner

$^1/_2$ cup each tomato and cucumber slices, drizzled with balsamic vinegar

Mussels Meurniere (Heat 1 teaspoon oil and $^1/_4$ cup each white wine and clam juice; sauté 1 shredded clove garlic, $^1/_2$ cup each chopped onions and tomatoes, and 2 teaspoons dry parsley. Add 2 ounces mussels; cook over medium heat, about 5 minutes. Serve over 1 cup pasta.) (6)

6 *POINTS*

Snack

$^1/_2$ cup warm apple cider (1)

1 slice frozen pumpkin pie, heated (6)

7 *POINTS*

TOTAL FOR THE DAY: 27 *POINTS*

SATURDAY

Breakfast

2 frozen blintzes, cooked, with 1 tablespoon fat-free sour cream (4)
1 cup cherries (1)
1 cup fat-free milk (2)
7 POINTS

Lunch

3 Buffalo wings (9)
$^1/_2$ cup each celery and carrot sticks (0)
$^1/_4$ cup fat-free blue cheese dressing (2)
4 short bread sticks (1)
12 POINTS

Dinner

Roasted Veggies (Toss $^1/_4$ sliced eggplant, $^1/_2$ red pepper, $^1/_2$ onion,
6 mushrooms, 1 tomato, and 1 shredded garlic clove with
2 teaspoons olive oil and 1 tablespoon rosemary; arrange on a
baking sheet and roast at 375°F for 30 minutes. Serve over 1 cup
whole wheat couscous, drizzled with balsamic vinegar.) (5)
5 POINTS

Snack

23 pretzel sticks (1)
1 cup aspartame-sweetened coffee nonfat yogurt (2)
3 POINTS

TOTAL FOR THE DAY: 27 POINTS

SUNDAY

Breakfast

1 small sesame bagel with 2 tablespoons light cream cheese,
1 ounce lox, 1 slice tomato, and 1 slice Bermuda onion and 1 lemon
wedge (5)
Orange Fizz (Mix ½ cup orange juice and ½ cup seltzer in a
glass.) (1)
1 cup fat-free milk (2)
8 POINTS

Lunch

Hummus Wrap (In a food processor, puree 2.5 ounces cooked
chickpeas, 2 tablespoons chickpea liquid, ¼ teaspoon shredded garlic, 1 teaspoon lemon juice, ½ teaspoon olive oil, and 1 tablespoon
canned tahini; spoon onto 1 whole-wheat mountain bread. Top
with 1 grated carrot, ½ cup chopped cucumbers, one slice onion,
and one slice tomato; roll up.) (6)
1 kiwi (1)
7 POINTS

Dinner

2 ounces cooked lean pork brushed with ¼ cup barbecue sauce (4)
1 small ear corn (1)
Garlicky Broccoli Rabe (Sauté 1 shredded garlic clove and 1 cup
broccoli rabe in 1 teaspoon oil until broccoli rabe is just wilted.) (1)
6 POINTS

Snack

1 slice angel food cake (2)
1 cup fat-free milk (2)
4 POINTS

TOTAL FOR THE DAY: 25 POINTS

WEEK 3

MONDAY

Breakfast

1 small fat-free bran muffin (2)
1 cup blueberries with 1 cup nonfat vanilla yogurt (4)
1 cup orange juice (2)
8 *POINTS*

Lunch

Grilled Orange-Chicken Salad (Arrange 3 ounces grilled chicken
breast, 1 chopped orange, and 4 red onion slices on 3 cups mesclun
lettuce.) (4)
Orange-Sesame Dressing (Mix 1 tablespoon each orange juice and
rice wine vinegar, 1 teaspoon each sesame oil and honey, and
$^1/_4$ teaspoon cinnamon; drizzle over salad.) (1)
1 small high-fiber whole grain roll (2)
7 *POINTS*

Dinner

Broccoli and Pesto Pasta (Toss 1 cup whole-wheat spaghetti with
2 tablespoons pesto sauce and 1 cup broccoli florets.) (6)
6 *POINTS*

Snack

2 coconut macaroons (2)
Nutty Cocoa (Heat 1 cup fat-free milk; stir in 1 teaspoon cocoa,
1 teaspoon aspartame, and a sprinkle of nutmeg.) (2)
4 *POINTS*

TOTAL FOR THE DAY: 25 *POINTS*

TUESDAY

Breakfast

1 cup toasted oat cereal with 1 cup fat-free milk and 1 sliced banana (6)
6 *POINTS*

Lunch

2 slices pumpernickel (4)
2 ounces honey ham (3)
³/₄ ounce low-fat cheddar cheese (2)
Lettuce leaves
Honey-Mustard Sandwich Butter (Mix 1 teaspoon each honey, mustard, and butter; spread on sandwiches.)
12 cherry tomatoes (0)
1 cup fat-free milk (2)
12 *POINTS*

Dinner

Tuscan Shrimp (Sauté ¹/₂ cup each chopped onions, mushrooms, tomatoes, and red peppers in 1 teaspoon olive oil and ¹/₄ cup chicken broth; add 4 ounces cooked shrimp, ¹/₂ cup cooked white beans, and garlic powder, rosemary, parsley, and lemon juice, to taste.) (5)
5 *POINTS*

Snack

¹/₂ grapefruit (1)
2 caramel-flavor rice cakes (2)
3 *POINTS*

TOTAL FOR THE DAY: 26 *POINTS*

WEDNESDAY

Breakfast

Corn Fritters (Whisk together 1 egg , 2 tablespoons fat-free milk,
1 tablespoon flour, and $1/4$ cup corn kernels; fry in 1 teaspoon
butter.) (3)
1 cup fat-free milk (2)
1 tangerine (1)
6 *POINTS*

Lunch

Tomato Tart (Layer 1 sliced beefsteak tomato, $1/2$ small sliced
Bermuda onion, $1/4$ cup nonfat Parmesan cheese, and 2 teaspoons
thyme on a large whole wheat pita; bake at 375°F for 20 minutes.)
(6)
1 cup aspartame-sweetened raspberry nonfat yogurt (2)
8 *POINTS*

Dinner

Pork with Cabbage and Apples (Brown 1 lean pork chop in
1 teaspoon oil; add $1/2$ cup each shredded cabbage, carrots, and
onions, $1/3$ cup apple juice, 2 teaspoons vinegar, and 1 sliced
green apple; bring to a boil and simmer for 5 minutes.) (6)
1 cup brown rice (4)
9 *POINTS*

Snack

$1/2$ small cinnamon-raisin bagel with 2 teaspoons apple butter (2)
2 *POINTS*

TOTAL FOR THE DAY: 25 *POINTS*

THURSDAY

Breakfast

1 small (2 ounce) blueberry muffin (3)
Tropical Smoothie (In a blender, puree $^1/_2$ frozen banana, $^1/_2$ cup pineapple juice, and 1 cup nonfat plain yogurt.) (5)
8 *POINTS*

Lunch

2 slices rye (4)
2 ounces turkey pastrami (4)
1 tablespoon mustard (0)
1 cup mixed greens with $^1/_2$ cup each diced tomatoes and cucumbers, $^1/_4$ cup shredded carrots, and 2 tablespoons fat-free ranch dressing (1)
1 cup fat-free milk (2)
11 *POINTS*

Dinner

Polenta with Sausage & Veggies (Sauté $^1/_4$ cup each chopped onions and red peppers in $^1/_4$ cup vegetable broth; stir in 1 cup broccoli rabe and garlic powder, to taste. When broccoli rabe is wilted, add 2 ounces low-fat cooked Italian sausage; spoon over $^1/_4$ cup cooked polenta.) (6)
6 *POINTS*

Snack

1 ounce fat-free bagel chips (2)
1 cup tomato juice (0)
2 *POINTS*

TOTAL FOR THE DAY: 27 *POINTS*

FRIDAY

Breakfast

1 cup shredded wheat with 1 cup fat-free milk and 1 sliced nectarine (5)
5 *POINTS*

Lunch

School Days PB&J (Spread 2 tablespoons peanut butter and 1 tablespoon grape jam on 2 slices high-fiber bread.) (7)
1 cup fat-free milk (2)
$^1/_2$ cup each celery and carrot sticks (0)
9 *POINTS*

Dinner

Crab Cake Casserole (Mix together $^1/_2$ cup canned crabmeat, $^1/_2$ chopped hard-boiled egg, 1 tablespoon fat-free mayonnaise, $^1/_2$ tablespoon lemon juice, $^1/_4$ teaspoon each Worcestershire and dry mustard, and salt and pepper, to taste. Combine 2 teaspoons melted butter, 1 tablespoon bread crumbs, and $^1/_4$ teaspoon baking powder; sprinkle over crab mixture and dust with paprika. Bake at 325°F until golden brown.) (5)
Gingered Vegetables (Melt 2 teaspoons butter in a saucepan. Stir in 1 teaspoon each grated ginger, honey, and lemon juice, and $^1/_4$ cup chicken broth; simmer. Pour over $^1/_2$ cup each steamed baby carrots and Brussels sprouts.) (2)
1 cup cubed watermelon (1)
8 *POINTS*

Snack

1 pear (1)
1 *POINT*

TOTAL FOR THE DAY: 23 *POINTS*

SATURDAY

Breakfast

Cinnamon-Raisin French Toast (Dip 2 slices cinnamon-raisin bread in mixture of 1 egg and $^1/_2$ cup fat-free milk; fry in 2 teaspoons butter until golden brown. Top with 1 tablespoon maple syrup.) (10)
1 cup fat-free milk (2)
$^1/_2$ cup orange juice (1)
13 *POINTS*

Lunch

Burger Classic (Layer a 3-ounce lean turkey burger on a high-fiber whole-wheat roll with lettuce, tomato, onion, and mustard.) (6)
1 cup carrot coins (0)
1 cup fat-free milk (2)
8 *POINTS*

Dinner

Vegetable Couscous (Sauté 1 small chopped onion, 1 cup mushrooms, and $^1/_2$ cup each diced zucchini and summer squash in $^1/_4$ cup vegetable broth until al dente, about 4 minutes. Add $^1/_2$ cup tomato sauce and season with garlic and basil. Stir into 1 cup cooked whole-wheat couscous and sprinkle with 2 tablespoons fat-free Parmesan cheese.) (5)
5 *POINTS*

Snack

1 frozen fruit juice bar (1)
1 *POINT*

TOTAL FOR THE DAY: 27 *POINTS*

SUNDAY

Breakfast

1 vegetarian breakfast patty (1)
1 small biscuit (2)
1 cup cantaloupe chunks with 1 cup nonfat vanilla yogurt (4)
7 POINTS

Lunch

1 large baked potato stuffed with $1/2$ cup each steamed broccoli and cauliflower (3)
Cheese Sauce (Melt 2 teaspoons butter in a saucepan; stir in 2 teaspoons flour, a dash of salt, and $1/3$ cup fat-free milk. Add 3 tablespoons shredded low-fat cheddar cheese; stir until smooth and pour over potato.) (5)
1 cup raspberries (1)
9 POINTS

Dinner

2 ounces lean cooked beef (3)
Barley and Wild Mushrooms (Sauté $1/4$ cup chopped onions in $1/4$ cup beef broth; add 1 cup frozen wild mushrooms, 1 teaspoon each rosemary and parsley, and $1/2$ cup cooked barley. When liquid is absorbed, add 1 tablespoon fat-free sour cream, and salt and pepper, to taste.) (1)
1 cup steamed haricots verts (0)
1 cup fat-free milk (2)
6 POINTS

Snack

1 fat-free brownie with $1/2$ cup nonfat vanilla ice cream (4)
4 POINTS

TOTAL FOR THE DAY: 26 POINTS

WEEK 4

MONDAY

Breakfast

Breakfast Rice Pudding (Bring 1 cup fat-free milk , $^1/_2$ cup cooked brown rice, 1 chopped Granny Smith apple, 1 teaspoon each brown sugar and butter, 1 tablespoon raisins, and $^1/_2$ teaspoon each cinnamon and vanilla to a simmer in a saucepan.) (7)
7 *POINTS*

Lunch

1 cup split pea soup (4)
Panzanella Salad (Toss together 1 cup cubed, toasted Italian bread, 1 chopped tomato, 1 chopped yellow pepper, 6 large olives, 6 anchovies, $^1/_4$ cup chopped fresh basil, 1 clove shredded garlic, 1 tablespoon balsamic vinegar, and salt and pepper, to taste.) (6)
10 *POINTS*

Dinner

1 3-ounce chicken breast brushed with 1 tablespoon duck sauce; broiled (3)
1 baked sweet potato with 1 teaspoon butter (4)
1 cup steamed eggplant with 1 teaspoon hoisin sauce (0)
2 plums (1)
8 *POINTS*

Snack

1 cup aspartame-sweetened vanilla nonfat yogurt (2)
2 *POINTS*

TOTAL FOR THE DAY: 27 *POINTS*

TUESDAY

Breakfast

1 small carrot muffin with 2 tablespoons nonfat cream cheese (3)
Orange-Cream Shake (In a blender, puree 1 cup nonfat aspartame-sweetened vanilla yogurt, $1/2$ frozen banana and $1/2$ cup orange juice.) (4)
7 *POINTS*

Lunch

2 slices reduced-calorie white bread (1)
2 ounces fat-free bologna (1)
1 tablespoon fat-free mayonnaise (0)
Lettuce leaves (0)
1 cup steamed broccoli (0)
2 *POINTS*

Dinner

Tofu Stir-Fry (In 2 teaspoons sesame oil, stir-fry: 1 tablespoon each minced garlic and ginger; 1 chopped green onion; 1 julienned carrot; $1/2$ cup each sliced mushrooms, sprouts, and snow peas; $1/3$ cup low-fat tofu; and 1 tablespoon each teriyaki sauce and orange juice.) (3)
1 cup sushi rice (5)
1 small glass white wine (2)
10 *POINTS*

Snack

2 graham crackers with 1 tablespoon peanut butter (3)
1 cup fat-free milk (2)
5 *POINTS*

TOTAL FOR THE DAY: 24 *POINTS*

WEDNESDAY

Breakfast

1 poached egg (2)
1 slice whole-wheat toast (2)
1 cup honeydew drizzled with lime juice (1)
1 cup fat-free milk (2)
7 *POINTS*

Lunch

Southern Mac and Cheese (Stir 1 cup steamed collard greens and
1 slice crumbled, crisp-cooked bacon into 1 cup cooked frozen
macaroni and cheese.) (7)
1 cup red and green grapes (1)
8 *POINTS*

Dinner

Salmon Salad (Toss 3 cups romaine lettuce with 1 teaspoon each
olive oil, honey, and basil, and 1 tablespoon lemon juice; top with a
3-ounce grilled salmon fillet and $^3/_4$ ounce low-fat feta cheese.) (6.5)
3 long sesame breadsticks (1.5)
8 *POINTS*

Snack

1 cup nonfat coffee yogurt (3)
3 *POINTS*

TOTAL FOR THE DAY: 26 *POINTS*

THURSDAY

Breakfast

1 3-inch cinnamon bun (5)
$^1/_2$ sliced papaya with 1 cup plain nonfat yogurt, drizzled with
1 teaspoon honey (4)
9 *POINTS*

Lunch

Zucchini Sandwich (Sauté $^1/_8$ cup chopped onions and $^1/_4$ teaspoon
each basil, oregano, and salt in 2 teaspoons oil until onion is translu-
cent. Add $^1/_2$ cup diced zucchini and spoon onto 1 slice high-fiber
whole-grain bread; top with $^1/_2$ cup chopped tomatoes and
$^3/_4$ ounce crumbled goat cheese.) (5)
1 cup raspberries with $^1/_4$ cup whipped topping (2)
7 *POINTS*

Dinner

Chicken Noodle Soup (Add 1 cup chopped onions, 2 sliced carrots,
a 3-ounce skinless chicken thigh, 1 tablespoon chopped parsley,
$1^1/_2$ ounces pasta shells, and salt and pepper, to taste, to 3 cups
boiling water; simmer for 10 minutes.) (6)
6 *POINTS*

Snack

Cappuccino made with 1 cup fat-free milk (2)
2 small fat-free chocolate biscotti (2)
4 *POINTS*

TOTAL FOR THE DAY: 26 *POINTS*

FRIDAY

Breakfast

1 1/2 cups puffed rice cereal (1)
1 cup fat-free milk (2)
1 cup strawberries (1)
4 POINTS

Lunch

2 cups mixed greens tossed with shredded carrots, radish slices, and
2 tablespoons fat-free French dressing (1)
1 frozen individual low-fat vegetable pot pie (8)
1 cup orange and grapefruit sections (1)
10 POINTS

Dinner

South of the Border Flounder (Sauté 1/2 diced onion and 1 clove
chopped garlic in 1 teaspoon oil; add 1 cup corn and 1/4 cup mild
salsa. Spoon over 3-ounce flounder fillet and bake at 375°F for
10 minutes.) (4)
1/2 cup brown rice mixed with 1/4 cup chopped cilantro (2)
6 POINTS

Snack

1 slice cinnamon-raisin bread with 1 cup aspartame-sweetened
apple pie–flavored nonfat yogurt (4)
4 POINTS

TOTAL FOR THE DAY: 24 POINTS

SATURDAY

Breakfast

2 ounces fat-free coffee cake (3)
1 cup blueberries and sliced peaches (1)
1 cup fat-free milk (2)
6 *POINTS*

Lunch

1 cup canned gazpacho (1)
2 ounces roast beef (4)
New Potato Salad (Toss 1 cup steamed diced new potatoes with
1/4 cup nonfat sour cream; 1 tablespoon each vinegar, parsley, and
chopped Bermuda onion; and salt and pepper, to taste.) (4)
9 *POINTS*

Dinner

Gado Gado (Arrange 1/2 cup cooked brown rice, 1/3 cup low-fat
tofu, 1 hard-cooked egg, 1/2 cup each steamed carrots, cabbage, and
green beans on a plate; drizzle with 1/4 cup bottled low-fat spicy
peanut sauce.) (7)
1 cup fat-free milk (2)
9 *POINTS*

Snack

Iced Cranberry Spritzer (Mix 1 cup cranberry juice, 1 cup seltzer, a
squeeze of lemon, and crushed ice in a tall glass.) (2)
2 *POINTS*

TOTAL FOR THE DAY: 26 *POINTS*

SUNDAY

Breakfast

Jack & Dill Omelet (Whisk together 1 egg, 2 tablespoons fat-free milk, 1 tablespoon flour, and 1 teaspoon snipped dill; cook in 1 teaspoon butter until firm, turning once. Arrange $^3/_4$ ounce low-fat Monterey Jack cheese and 4 asparagus spears on one half; fold over and sprinkle with salt, to taste.) (5)

$^1/_4$ cantaloupe (1)

6 *POINTS*

Lunch

1 cup canned black-eyed pea soup (2)

1 2-inch square piece corn bread (2)

1 cup unsweetened applesauce (1)

1 cup fat-free milk (2)

7 *POINTS*

Dinner

Mediterranean Chicken (Coat a skinless 3-ounce chicken thigh with mixture of 2 teaspoons each cornmeal and flour and $^1/_4$ teaspoon salt; brown in 2 teaspoons oil and remove from skillet. In same skillet, sauté $^1/_2$ cup each chopped onions, mushrooms, and green peppers (add vegetable broth if more liquid needed); add 8 ounces canned tomatoes, 6 large olives, 2 teaspoons each garlic powder and oregano. Return chicken thigh to the skillet and simmer 15 minutes.) (6)

1 cup cooked rigatoni (3)

9 *POINTS*

Snack

1 cup blackberries (1)

1 cup aspartame-sweetened blackberry nonfat yogurt (2)

3 *POINTS*

TOTAL FOR THE DAY: 25 *POINTS*

Index